Table of Contents

SLAVE MENTALITY

The Imaginary Shackles of a Victimized Society

By

Ling A. Gramling

This book is dedicated to:

Denice Himmel and Janet Massie

Also, thanks to the Porch Bandits!

Introduction

To begin, I'd like to thank each and every person who is, has, or is planning on reading this book. It is not my intention to educate anyone. I just want to point those who are interested, in the right direction. Educate yourself! Even though the subject matter, Victim Mentality is multifaceted, the information is still readily available. This will not be sugar-coated justifications for the paroles of being Black. Instead, it's a self-reflection of how Black people have been manipulated to embrace failure as a way of life.

It has become apparent to me that, even though the content of this book is not new found facts or evidence of that that needs to be publicized, that the sheer weight of truths and facts can be overwhelming for most people. We are living in an age where information is available but manipulation of information is also rampant and often times the simplest event is only explained in the most complex way. We may find ourselves straying away or digressing from a specific topic to a point where we aren't even interested anymore once we've realized it.

My greatest hope is that reading this book will make it easier to focus on the matter at hand while you, the reader, can research the material being presented. In educating yourself, you alleviate the possibility of adopting the writer's biases and learning the actual facts, not anyone's interpretation of them. Yes, we all have a tendency to lean one way or another.

Chapter One: A History of Slavery

The Origins

Most pundits would want you to believe that slavery was a product of early colonial America. In fact, the concept of slavery spans through many cultures and civilizations and was a ubiquitous institution.

Records of slavery date back to the Sumerians in the 5th or 6th millennium BC in ancient Mesopotamia. Most likely, it was a byproduct of the development of agriculture. With agriculture, came the stability to establish trade. Trade produced profits and debts. The first slaves were likely indentured servants who agreed to work without pay until their debt was settled. They were exclusively all men. As the practice becomes more commonplace, one lender may have sold his servant's labor to another lender to settle their debt or just for profit.

As the appetite for slavery became insatiable, the acquisition shifted to the spoils or war. Kings sent out bands of raiders to the nearby, less developed towns and cities for the acquisition of slaves. These slaves were undoubtedly needed to help further build the Sumerian empire. The defeated were sold, traded, resold, and used in any manner his owner saw fit. With the acceptance that slaves were considered livestock, like cows or horses, they now have no human worth. Slaves could be sent to their deaths in military excursions just as easily as being sent to their deaths by a consenting crowd for entertainment. They could be sent to perform manual labor until death just as easily as for sex trafficking. The concept of indentured servitude became chattel slavery when the idea that someone can physically own someone else for a lifetime beyond any debt settling or agreement to serve without pay for a finite amount of time. The combination of these practices and the change in attitude about the treatment of another human being in the same way livestock or equipment is treated paved the way for the development of slavery and slave trading.

It was the invention of the wheel and the sail that broadened the trade routes which, in turn, broadened the trading of slaves outside of Mesopotamia. The connection to the Arab, and later the Muslim states, opened up trade routes to Europe and Asia. Slave trading became a commonplace worldwide by which all parties contributed to, and prospered. As clans toppled clans and empires toppled empires, there were always enough slaves to rebuild and expand the economies of the triumphant. Throughout the history of mankind, no religion, culture or civilization can claim exclusion from slavery or the slave trade as a whole.

Slavery started with civilization and grew with every development thereafter. Every pocket of humanity had its form of slavery. Some were as cruel as we recognize it to be where slaves had no rights and were destined for a slow painful death while others gave their slaves rights and the ability to become citizens over a period of time. The Babylonian slaves, probably because of the indentured servant beginnings, were allowed to own property even though they were legally 3rd class citizens. Sparta and Greece were heavily dependent on slavery and had different methodologies. Sparta enslaved conquered states but allowed them to stay on their land while forcing them to labor for Sparta. The Greek slaves, on the other hand, had a range of possibilities. They could die from laboring in the mines or become a part of the Greek elite police force and were rewarded with certain privileges.

The Expansion

Slavery in the 1st century was a pervasive and deeply entrenched institution in various parts of the world, shaped by the cultural, economic, and social dynamics of the time. During this period, different regions had distinct systems of slavery, and the experiences of enslaved individuals varied significantly. There were diverse features of slavery in the 1st century across different civilizations. The slave trade expanded to all corners of the world. Europe traded slaves with Africa, Asia, and South America. The Vikings, known for conquering empires, were very plenteously involved slave traders in Europe. Viking conquests spanned from the Nordic countries such as Denmark, Finland, Iceland, and Sweden to as far west as North America. Their conquests reached the Mediterranean empires in Spain and North Africa. They've even reached the highly embattled Constantinople, otherwise known as Istanbul. European slaves, acquired from victories, were a regular part of their traded goods in the European theatre. The Roman and Greek Empires were also active slave traders in the same theatre.

One of the most well-documented instances of slavery in the 1st century was in the Roman Empire. Slavery played a vital role in the Roman economy and society. Enslaved people in Rome came from a diversity of origins, with many coming from the results of conquered regions. Slaves were used for various purposes, from working on agricultural estates and in mines to performing domestic and administrative tasks. The ownership of slaves was a status symbol, and wealthy Romans often possessed a considerable number of enslaved individuals. Slavery in Rome was based on the idea that enslaved people were "property" with limited legal rights. However, there were some opportunities for slaves to gain their freedom, and they could even become Roman citizens after being emancipated by their owners.

In the Eastern Mediterranean, the Hellenistic period in the 1st century also had its own forms of slavery. Slavery was prevalent in the city-states and kingdoms that emerged after the conquests of Alexander the Great. Similar to the Roman world, people enslaved had varying roles in society, from agricultural labor to domestic service. Greek slavery was deeply embedded in the culture, with philosophical discussions about the ethics of slavery and the treatment of enslaved people. Some philosophers like Aristotle justified slavery as a natural and necessary institution. He wrote that natural slaves were slaves because their souls were not complete and that they lacked certain qualities, such as the ability to think properly, and so they needed to have masters to tell them what to do. He made a direct comparison to owning pets.

Slavery also existed in China although it may have been slightly different compared to the Western world. The concept of slavery in China was often tied to the state and its bureaucracy. Enslaved individuals could be prisoners of war, criminals, or those who had fallen into debt. The Chinese state sometimes used forced labor for monumental construction projects, such as the construction of the Great Wall. Slavery in China was less about chattel slavery and more about state control over them, as they often retained some social and legal rights.

India, in the 1st century, had a complex social hierarchy that included various forms of unfree labor. The caste system, which categorized people into different groups based on occupation and birth, sometimes confined people to hereditary forms of servitude. Bonded labor, debt slavery, and the exploitation of low-caste people were prevalent. Enslaved people in India had limited opportunities to change their social status and were often trapped in a cycle of servitude. This system not only dictated social interactions but also played a crucial role in shaping economic and labor relations. One significant aspect of this complex social structure was the existence of various forms of unfree labor. Unfree labor, otherwise known as slave labor, refers to situations where individuals are compelled to work against their will, often with limited rights and opportunities for personal advancement. In the context of ancient India, this took several forms, contributing to a hierarchical and stratified society. Bonded labor and debt slavery were prevalent forms of unfree labor in ancient India. Economic circumstances often forced them into servitude, either through indebtedness or familial obligations. People would become bonded laborers, working to repay debts or fulfill obligations, and in many cases, these conditions persisted across generations.

In parts of Africa and the Middle East, slavery existed long before the 1st century. Enslavement was often a result of inter-tribal warfare, where those who were captured in conflict became slaves to the victorious. Slavery in these regions had a unique character, influenced by indigenous traditions and social structures. This process of enslavement resulting from inter-tribal warfare underscored the volatile nature of power dynamics in these regions. Those captured in the aftermath of conflict were often subjected to a life of servitude, contributing to the expansion of slave populations within these societies. The reasons behind inter-tribal warfare and subsequent enslavement were multifaceted, ranging from competition for resources to disputes over territory or ideological differences. One noteworthy aspect of slavery in these regions was its nuanced connection to indigenous traditions and social hierarchies. Unlike some other forms of slavery seen in different historical contexts, where social mobility was severely restricted, in certain African and Middle Eastern societies, there existed the potential for enslaved individuals to attain higher social status over time. This phenomenon could be influenced by a variety of factors, including loyalty, skills, or integration into the cultural and familial structures of the enslaving community. Some of the enslaved, however, did manage to navigate a trajectory that allowed them to rise above their initial status, demonstrating a fluidity in social positions that was not always present in other historical slave systems. This fluidity could be facilitated by factors such as acts of valor, allegiance, or the development of specific skills that were valued within the enslaving community.

The 1st century marked a time when various civilizations practiced slavery, each with its own distinct characteristics and justifications. It is crucial to acknowledge, however, that despite the differences in the justifications and practices of slavery, the common thread binding these societies was the horrific experience endured by the enslaved. Forced into labor and servitude against their will, these people faced formidable challenges, their lives dictated by the whims of their masters. The absence of agency often translated into limited opportunities for social mobility or freedom, perpetuating a cycle of exploitation and subjugation. The shared reality for those subjected to slavery during the 1st century was one of hardship, marked by a lack of autonomy and the constant struggle for basic human rights. The prevailing conditions of slavery during this period underscore the harsh and dehumanizing nature of an institution that transcended geographical and cultural boundaries.

The 2nd Century BC saw the end of Viking influence, making way for the rise of the Ottomans, whose reach extended predominantly across the Balkans and Eastern Europe, though their impact was not confined to these regions alone. The Ottoman Empire's expansion was characterized by conquest, and while the acquisition of slaves was a significant outcome of their campaigns, it was not the sole product. Particularly noteworthy was the activity of the Barbary Pirates under Ottoman control, who engaged in the kidnapping for ransom. Targeting merchant ships, which often doubled as passenger transports, these pirates seized women and children to be sold as slaves, while the men were held for ransom. If the demanded ransom was not met by the respective governments, enslavement became the alternative. The scope of Ottoman, Arab, and Barbary Muslim slave trading practices during this period was extensive, with over 7 million Europeans falling victim to these activities. The Barbary Pirates, acting as corsairs along the North African coast, created a climate of fear and uncertainty for Mediterranean sailors and coastal communities. The impact of this form of slavery extended beyond the immediate regions of the Ottoman Empire, illustrating the interconnectedness of global trade and the brutal consequences of maritime conflicts during this era.

Prior to the arrival of European settlers, the practice of slavery and the slave trade was already deeply entrenched in the cultures of indigenous peoples in North, Central, and South America. The Mayan and Aztec civilizations, for instance, maintained meticulous ledgers documenting slave trades that spanned centuries, well before the arrival of the first Europeans on their shores. Notably, several North American tribes, including the Illinois and the Ottawa, were actively engaged in this practice, showcasing the prevalence and diversity of indigenous approaches to slavery. This approach exhibited a broader scope of acquisition. In addition to traditional forms of enslavement, indigenous peoples sometimes resorted to selling women and children in exchange for food or other essential supplies. The motivations for engaging in such practices were multifaceted, ranging from economic considerations to social and cultural factors. In some cases, the acquisition of slaves became a symbolic act, a means for them or the tribes to assert their warrior status or undergo a rite of passage.

Religion also played a significant role in shaping the practice of slavery among indigenous civilizations. For instance, in the case of the Aztec civilization, religious beliefs influenced various aspects of society, including the institution of slavery. The complex interplay between cultural, economic, and religious factors underscores the diversity of indigenous approaches to slavery in the Americas before European colonization. It is evident that the dynamics of these approaches were shaped by a combination of economic necessities, cultural norms, and spiritual beliefs. The multifaceted nature of these practices highlights the complexity of the indigenous societies in the Americas, before European influence, and challenges simplistic narratives about the history of slavery in the region.

The arrival of early European settlers brought a significant shift in the dynamics of the indigenous slave trade in the Americas. Initially, indigenous peoples engaged in trade, including the exchange of slaves, with the newcomers. However, the situation soon transformed as the Europeans actively participated in and eventually took control of the slave trade. This transition was facilitated by the Europeans supplying arms to indigenous groups, enabling them to conduct more efficient raids on nearby tribes for the purpose of procuring slaves. These raids were not limited to indigenous communities; early European settlements themselves became targets. The introduction of firearms by Europeans altered the power dynamics among indigenous groups, intensifying intertribal conflicts and increasing the scale of slave raids. The expansion of the slave trade became intertwined with the broader European colonial project, reinforcing the economic and social structures that sustained the institution of slavery.

As the relationship between Europeans and indigenous peoples evolved, the devastating impact of European diseases on the native populations became a significant factor. The introduction of diseases like smallpox, brought by the Europeans, led to widespread sickness and death among the indigenous communities. This demographic decline posed a threat to the indigenous slave trade, as the labor force necessary for sustaining it dwindled. In direct response to this challenge, Europeans shifted their focus to a different source of labor, African slaves. The transatlantic slave trade emerged as a lucrative alternative, and the demand for African laborers increased significantly. This transition marked a critical juncture in the history of slavery in the

Americas, as the exploitation of African slaves became central to the economic and social structures of European colonies. The convergence of European colonization, the supply of firearms, the impact of diseases, and the subsequent turn to African slavery all contributed to a complex and deeply troubling chapter in the history of the Americas.

The Atlantic Slave Trade

The Atlantic slave trade, also known as the Transatlantic slave trade, refers to the enforced transportation of African people to the Americas, primarily during the 15th to the 19th centuries. This tragic episode stands as a dark chapter in the annals of human history, marked by the exploitation, suffering, and degradation of millions of people. Driven by economic interests, racism, and the quest for power, the Atlantic slave trade left an indelible mark on the continents involved. The roots of the Atlantic slave trade can be traced back to the Age of Exploration, a period characterized by European powers' search for new routes to Asia. In the process, they encountered the African continent. The Portuguese were pioneers in this endeavor, purchasing African slaves as early as the mid-15th century. Subsequently, other European nations, including the Spanish, Dutch, English, and French, became deeply involved in the trade. The initial motivations for purchasing African slaves included labor for the burgeoning sugar plantations in the Atlantic islands and later in the North and South American colonies. The oldest colonies in the United States were the Spanish colonies in what would now be St. Augustine Florida. Though originally, they enslaved the indigenous tribes, the Spanish soon abolished this practice in the early 16th century removing the indigenous people from slavery and replacing them with enslaved Africans starting in South America and then slowly adopting it in the colonies of Florida.

The arrival of the British brought continued enslavement of the indigenous people along the East Coast as well as a drastic increase in the African slave trade. The Dutch were most efficient in providing African slaves for the markets in the New World. The slave trade became a juggernaut in the economy of both the North and the South. Dominant were the sugar cane and cotton industries. So ingrained was the slave trade that even after slavery was outlawed in the North, the act of slave trading was not. Merchant ships from northern companies still supplied the South with the supply of slaves to maintain or expand their economies. The institution of slavery has become deeply ingrained in the socio-economic fabric of the American colonies. Despite the abolition of slavery in the North, the practice of slave trading persisted. Even after legislative measures were taken to outlaw slavery in Northern states, the act of slave trading itself was not universally prohibited. Merchant ships from Northern companies continued to play a pivotal role in supplying the South with enslaved people, serving to sustain and expand the Southern economies that were heavily reliant on slave labor. The economic significance of the slave trade was particularly pronounced in the Southern colonies, where large-scale plantations depended on the labor-intensive cultivation of crops like sugar cane and cotton. The profitability of these industries rested on the exploitation of enslaved people, leading to the perpetuation of the slave trade even in the face of changing legal landscapes. This complex and morally reprehensible system highlights the entwined relationship between economic interests and the perpetuation of slavery. The historical legacy of the slave trade, both in terms of its impact on individuals and the shaping of regional economies, underscores the profound and enduring consequences of this dark chapter in American history.

The Industrial Revolution played a pivotal role by acting as a catalyst for the beginning of the end of slavery in the United States. This transformative period, which emerged in the late 18th century, saw a shift from agricultural economies to industrialized and mechanized production. The adoption of machines for various tasks meant that the cost of labor became more economically feasible using machinery than relying on human labor. As European countries gradually recognized the economic advantages of industrialization, many began to abolish slavery in the late 18th century. In the United States, however, the transition away from slavery took longer to materialize. It wasn't until the mid-19th century that the country started to follow suit. The North Atlantic Slave Trade, which had been a fundamental part of the American economic and social landscape, was on the brink of extinction. The economic and social structures in the Southern states, heavily reliant on slave labor in the agricultural sector, resisted this change more vehemently.

During the 18th and 19th centuries, abolitionist movements gained significant momentum, especially in Europe, spearheaded by prominent figures such as William Wilberforce. As an English politician and philanthropist, Wilberforce played a crucial role in advocating for the abolition of the slave trade. Concurrently, organizations like the Society for Effecting the Abolition of the Slave Trade were instrumental in channeling efforts toward the eradication of this inhumane practice. The abolitionist movement was characterized by a convergence of moral and economic motivations. Morally, for example, a growing number of people within society began to recognize the inherent moral indefensibility of slavery. Philosophical and moral arguments against the institution gained traction, fueled by Enlightenment ideals and a burgeoning sense of human rights. Abolitionists argued that every individual, regardless of race, was entitled to the basic rights and dignity that enslavement denied. As narratives from formerly enslaved individuals and abolitionist literature spread, public sentiment shifted towards an increasing abhorrence of the human cost associated with the slave trade.

Economic considerations played a pivotal role in the momentum of the abolitionist movement. Abolitionists argued that slavery was not only morally reprehensible but also economically inefficient in the long run. While slave labor may have been economically advantageous in the short term, the long-term costs, both in terms of human suffering and potential social unrest, were deemed unsustainable. The economic inefficiency of slavery became increasingly apparent as industrialization gained momentum, highlighting the potential for alternative forms of labor that did not rely on the exploitation of human beings. Still, it demanded the combined force of moral conviction and economic reasoning to propel the abolitionist movements to achieve significant milestones. The eventual success of these movements led to legislative measures and policies that sought to dismantle the slave trade and, eventually, slavery itself. The British Parliament passed the Abolition of the Slave Trade Act in 1807, making it illegal to engage in the transatlantic slave trade. The efforts of figures like William Wilberforce, who was a sponsor of the Slavery Abolition Act of 1833, and the collective endeavors of other abolitionist organizations marked a turning point in history, showcasing the power of grassroots movements to effect substantial social and legal change.

The abolition of slavery in the United States was a landmark event in the mid-19th century, marked by two significant milestones. The first was the issuance of the Emancipation Proclamation by President Abraham Lincoln in 1863, during the throes of the Civil War. This executive order declared all slaves in Confederate-held territory to be free, a crucial step towards dismantling the institution of slavery in the United States. The Emancipation Proclamation, however, had limitations, as its authority did not extend to regions under Union control. The second milestone came with the ratification of the 13th Amendment to the U.S. Constitution in 1865, which formally abolished slavery throughout the entire United States, transcending the limitations of the Emancipation Proclamation. This amendment, coming in the aftermath of the Civil War, symbolized a definitive break from the institution of slavery and laid the groundwork for the United States to move toward equality and prosperity, despite the challenges that persisted during the Reconstruction era. The industrialization of the economy, coupled with political and social changes, played a critical role in bringing about the eventual end of slavery in the United States.

Simultaneously, most of Europe was also undergoing significant shifts in their stance on slavery during the 19th century. France and the Netherlands, among others, took steps to abolish the slave trade and, subsequently, slavery itself in their colonies. The 19th century witnessed a gradual shift in global attitudes towards the institution of slavery, driven by evolving moral sensibilities, economic considerations, and changing social norms. European nations, influenced by Enlightenment ideals and a growing awareness of human rights, moved towards recognizing the moral indefensibility of enslavement and taking legislative actions to bring about its end. These collective efforts reflected an emerging global consensus against the institution of slavery, signaling a broader movement toward recognizing the fundamental rights and dignity of all individuals. The abolition of slavery in the United States and European colonies marked a turning point in history by challenging deeply entrenched practices and world economic norms. While slavery continues to influence some societies today, the abolitionist movements of the 19th century set important precedents for human rights and justice.

Between the years 1525 and 1866, the transatlantic slave trade left an indelible mark on history, witnessing the forced migration of approximately 10.7 million enslaved Africans to the New World. This staggering number encapsulates the immense human suffering and exploitation endured by people who were forcibly uprooted from their homelands and subjected to the brutality of the transatlantic voyage. Within this broader context, about 390,000 enslaved Africans were transported to North America, a region that would later merge into the United States. It is crucial to recognize that these numbers only represent those who survived the grueling journey, as a significant number perished due to the deplorable conditions aboard the slave ships. The absence of a requirement to document slave births during this period adds a layer of complexity to understanding the total number of people who were enslaved. The lack of comprehensive birth records makes it difficult for historians to accurately estimate the total enslaved population. Consequently, we are left to make educated guesses and approximations, highlighting the inadequacy of historical documentation when it comes to capturing the full scope of the human tragedy that was the transatlantic slave trade. It is quite a challenge to fully recognize the full extent of the impact of slavery when depending on incomplete historical records.

Nevertheless, the enormity of these numbers serves as a rather distressing reminder of the scale of human suffering and the deep scars left by the transatlantic slave trade. It underscores the necessity of acknowledging the historical injustices endured by those who were enslaved and the profound impact that this dark chapter has had on the shaping of societies in the New World. Understanding the scale of the transatlantic slave trade is crucial for confronting the historical legacy of slave mentality and victim mentality to better understand why people make the choices they make and work towards breaking the constraints so that all can be truly free.

Final Thoughts

Slavery started with the first civilization and grew with every economic development thereafter. Every pocket of humanity had its form of slavery starting with enslaving their own people. Some were as cruel as we recognize them to be where slaves had no rights and were destined for a slow painful death while others gave their slaves rights and the ability to become citizens of the society that enslaved them.

The Atlantic slave trade represents a profound and dark chapter in human history. It was characterized by the brutal exploitation and dehumanization of millions of Africans, leading to far-reaching impacts on Africa, the Americas, and Europe. The trade eventually succumbed to the efforts of abolitionists and the resistance of the enslaved, marking a turning point in the long history of slavery. While the Atlantic slave trade has left deep scars, it also serves as a reminder of the resilience and strength of those who fought against this inhumane system and the ongoing struggle for justice and equality in the modern world.

The heinous institution of slavery left an enduring impact on the physical, mental, and emotional well-being of its survivors, an impact that reverberates through generations. The trauma inflicted during centuries of enslavement has created a complex web of generational mindsets, influencing both the descendants of those who were enslaved and the broader societies they inhabit. By exploring the generational mindset of the slaves, perhaps we will unveil a legacy of resilience, strength, and cultural continuity. In the face of unimaginable adversity, enslaved individuals often developed coping mechanisms, community bonds, and cultural practices that served as a source of identity and solidarity. These resilient aspects of the generational mindset became crucial components of the survival and preservation of cultural heritage.

The freed descendants of slaves inherited a complex legacy. Despite the abolition of slavery, they faced enduring challenges such as systemic racism, segregation, and economic disparities that impeded their full integration into society. The generational trauma of slavery persisted through discriminatory practices, limiting access to education, employment opportunities, and equal representation. The psychological burdens carried by descendants of slaves have influenced self-perception, identity formation, and collective consciousness. Moreover, the lasting repercussions of slavery extend beyond personal experiences to societal structures and norms. Generational mindsets shaped by the trauma of ancestral enslavement contribute to persistent inequalities, racial disparities, and systemic injustices. These deep-seated issues are reflected in areas such as education, healthcare, criminal justice, and economic opportunities, creating a cycle that reinforces and perpetuates the consequences of historical injustices. Acknowledging and addressing the generational mindset born out of slavery is a crucial step toward dismantling the entrenched structures of inequality. It involves not only confronting the historical trauma but also actively working towards dismantling systemic injustices that perpetuate the negative legacies of the past. By fostering awareness, advocating for equality, and promoting social justice, society can contribute to breaking the cycle of generational trauma and building a more inclusive and empathetic future...but do these circumstances really exist? Could the trauma have caused a generational restriction of the idea of freedom? Are current atrocities mere mental shackles or are they objectively tangible? Since Black people were not the only slaves, does it affect other ethnic groups as well?

Chapter Two: What is The Slave Mentality?

Define and Describe

One definition of slavery is a person who is the property of and wholly subject to another; a bond servant. If we combine that with the state of one's mind, one's views, or one's outlook, we would get a glimpse into understanding what Slave Mentality is, or at the very least, how it could be defined. It would be safe to describe Slave Mentality as the conditioning of a person's mind to accept circumstances that are not safe and comfortable. It causes the mind to reject free will and embrace low self-esteem. It imposes the thoughts and opinions of the "master" onto the slave. It causes the inability to imagine life without the "master". It enhances the "master's" demagoguery to the point of perceiving anyone contradicting the "master' as an enemy who is out to destroy their life and livelihood. This condition causes delusional manifestations of shackles that encourage illiteracy, indebtedness, vilification of education, and an unconcealed rejection of those who are educated. Slave mentality robs its victims of the ability to reason and entices them to feel like slavery is right and they should praise their master for allowing them and their families to work.

Perhaps another description would be the feeling of being defeated. We all recognize the feeling of defeat for a particular situation or a life event that may last several months or several years. What we cannot fathom is the feeling of being defeated permanently. We would have to accept that there is no way out, no short- or long-term solution, and no savior will come to deliver us from this evil. To take it even further, we would have to understand that this defeat is generational. Our children and grandchildren will be born and raised in defeat and we are incapable of changing that fate. This must be what every person who was enslaved had to have thought at some point or another. Once this personal truth has been accepted, we stop looking for solutions and start adapting to the world in which we live. This dichotomy between master and slave had to be enforced and maintained by the master and accepted and maintained by the slave.

We can take a lesson on Slave Mentality from the Bible as well. Moses freed the slaves and led them out of Egypt. They were destined to establish their own nation. However, the book of Numbers and the book of John describe how after being freed, many wanted to go back into slavery because they perceived it as a better and easier way of life. They would rather live in servitude for a perceived benefit as opposed to being free to determine their own life. They even refused to take the land that was promised to them. We could deduce that Slave Mentality was the reason for their early demise. They were incapable of understanding what freedom means and were willing to return to slavery. We also learn from the Bible that it was generational. The Israelites who took the journey, taught it to the children so that generations thereafter, they were still yearning to live under servitude than to be free.

Willie Lynch Syndrome

It is believed that one man was able to understand the methodology to make slavery flourish. He spread his ideas to the American slave owners on how to break slaves and make them willfully conform to servitude. He understood the mental aspect of slavery and how it could benefit all slave owners. His speech, though historically debated for its authenticity, symbolizes the insidious nature of tactics employed to perpetuate racial hierarchies and maintain social control during the era of slavery. The strategies he proposed, aimed at sowing discord and fostering distrust among enslaved communities, contributed to the deep-seated divisions that persist in contemporary society. The psychological scars inflicted by these methods have endured through generations, influencing the ways in which individuals perceive themselves and each other within racial and cultural contexts.

Willie Lynch, a British slave owner from Jamaica, delivered a notorious speech on the banks of the James River in Virginia, where he was invited to instruct Virginian slave owners in methods of managing their enslaved population. This speech, often referred to as the "Willie Lynch Letter," outlined strategies to control and manipulate enslaved individuals, emphasizing the use of division and psychological tactics to maintain dominance. Lynch's methods were designed to create a perpetual system of control, pitting slaves against each other based on factors like age, gender, and complexion. The term "lynching," now associated with racially motivated violence and brutality, ironically finds its origin in Willie Lynch's name.

"In my bag here, I have a foolproof method for controlling your Black slaves. I guarantee every one of you that if it is installed correctly, it will control the slaves for at least 300 years. My method is simple. Any member of your family or your overseer can use it," was the start of his sermon on the river's bank. He goes on to say that Fear, Distrust, and Envy were the tools he used in amplifying the difference between the slaves to control the slaves. By pitting the old against the young, the males against the females, and the lighter-skinned against the darker-skinned in an effort to make them distrust each other and only trust, love, and respect their master. Lynch proclaimed that if his methods were used intensely for one year, the slaves would perpetuate the distrust amongst themselves. His methodology would evolve into what is now called the Willie Lynch Syndrome. It would institutionalize the concept of making a particular group of people hate everything about themselves and accept the consequential low self-esteem that is inevitable when one has allowed mental capitulation.

While initially linked to the historical context of extrajudicial violence against African Americans during the post-Reconstruction era, the term, "lynching" has evolved to encompass broader meanings, representing not only physical violence but also systemic oppression and racial injustice. Understanding the origin of the term underscores the historical continuity of racial violence and the enduring impact of strategies devised to maintain social control. Addressing the legacy of Willie Lynch requires a commitment to dismantling systemic racism and fostering unity and understanding among diverse communities. Recognizing the historical roots of divisive tactics is essential for acknowledging the broader impact of racialized violence and inequality.

Fast forward to the modern day, we see that these practices have had a lasting effect on certain communities. As he predicted, the "slaves" are perpetuating the distrust amongst themselves and have passed that mistrust on through the generations. Focusing on the Black community, we can point out the rivalries between different neighborhoods or even different streets within the same neighborhood. The division is there and they are being perpetuated by the people in those communities. It is, by no means, a secret in the Black community that light and dark-skinned people are also in disapproval of each other. My personal favorite, of course, is the rift between those who are well educated and those who are not.

These behaviors are not characteristics of segments of just the Black community! Because of the omnipresence of slavery, segments of every ethnicity have had and are having the same experiences. Low-income communities of every ethnicity display these disruptive peculiarities. This is hardly to say that it is not present in affluent segments as well, but the affluent tend to be better educated and therefore have a higher self-esteem which breaks Willie Lynch Syndrome's hold on them.

Willie Lynch's concept of breaking down the major traditional institutions such as family, marriage, and religion as well as reversing the roles by establishing a strong woman to stand in front of the weak man is also still very present today. As he would have it, the strong male had to be destroyed in front of the woman so that her instinct to protect her progenies would deter her from raising mentally strong males, as she has witnessed their demise. She would also, inadvertently, raise psychologically independent females. This role reversal is designed to break down the traditional family structure and insert fear and mistrust into the family.

Fast forward to today. We see that the traditional family structure has been greatly damaged, particularly in the Black community. "The black family, which had survived centuries of slavery and discrimination, began rapidly disintegrating in the liberal welfare state that subsidized unwed pregnancy and changed welfare from an emergency rescue to a way of life." Thomas Sowell was contemptuous in his stance about the, presumably, unintended consequences of the Great Society which was the breakdown of the Black family. It is exactly his breakdown that resembles Lynch's enslavement strategy.

Thomas Sowell's observation on the transformation of the family structure within the black population in the United States encapsulates a critical social shift that unfolded over a specific period. In 1965, a predominant 76.4% of black children were born to married mothers, pointing to a prevailing trend of nuclear families within the black community during that era. This statistic not only reflects a demographic reality but also underscores the existence of stable, two-parent households among black families at the time. However, the landscape experienced a seismic change by 2009, as revealed by Sowell's data, which indicates that 73% of black children were born to unmarried mothers. This shift represents a substantial departure from the earlier trend and suggests a significant rise in single-parent households within the black community. The abrupt alteration in family structure prompts Sowell to characterize this phenomenon as a complete reversal of the progress made in restoring the Black family structure.

The reference to the era of slavery and the influence of Willie Lynch adds a historical dimension to Sowell's analysis. By invoking the historical context, Sowell implies that the shift in family structure is not merely a recent development but has roots that trace back to the legacy of slavery and the purported tactics of Willie Lynch. Willie Lynch, though historically contested as a figure, is often associated with strategies aimed at dividing and controlling slaves by disrupting familial bonds. Sowell suggests that the repercussions of such historical influences have endured and contributed to the contemporary challenges facing black families. His commentary underscores the broader implications of the observed shift. It goes beyond being a statistical change and is portrayed as a setback in the ongoing efforts to foster stable family units within the black community. By framing it as a "complete reversal," Sowell emphasizes the gravity of the transformation and its potential impact on the well-being and resilience of black families, linking it to both recent social changes and historical legacies.

Programs like the Children's Defense Fund made it easier for single mothers to receive government-sponsored programs like prenatal care, daycare, and other subsidies. These programs create the same environment of distrust and reversed roles as Lynch's macabre methodology. We can even take a few steps further in conformation of Lynch's prediction that if these practices are maintained long enough, Black people will perpetuate them. The Children's Defense Fund was created by Marian Wright Edelman, a graduate of Spelman College at Yale Law School. With all due respect for her achievements and noble advocacy for the underprivileged children, that does not lessen the unintended consequences of these programs. Economist Walter Williams stated, "The undeniable truth is that neither slavery nor Jim Crow nor the harshest racism has decimated the black family the way the welfare state has." Perhaps it is the welfare state that has adopted the methods of Willie lynch but has elevated it to the political level to perpetuate, but also, increase its reach on society creating and appeasing to a new generation of mentally enslaved people.

Stockholm Syndrome

Stockholm Syndrome can be defined as a complex psychological phenomenon in which hostages or victims of abduction develop a bond or positive emotional connection with their captors, as well as with their agenda and demands. It was first recognized after a bank robbery in Stockholm, Sweden, in 1973, where hostages began to empathize with their captors, this condition has since captured the fascination and curiosity of psychologists, criminologists, and the public. People susceptible to this condition may develop positive feelings towards their captors. In turn, they also develop negative feelings against those who may be trying to help them, even going as far as refusing to cooperate against their captors. They also begin to adopt their captors' goals and values. The precise causes of Stockholm Syndrome remain a subject of debate among psychologists and researchers. Several factors may contribute to the development of this phenomenon. Patty Hearst, granddaughter of publishing magnate William Randolph Hearst, was kidnapped by the Symbionese Liberation Army (SLA) in the United States., Colleen Stan, Mackenzie Phillips, Cleveland Captives, and Mary McElroy are perhaps the most famous examples of Stockholm Syndrome.

One of the central psychological mechanisms that can trigger Stockholm Syndrome is its role as a coping mechanism in situations of extreme stress, isolation, and captivity. When people are subjected to terrifying or potentially life-threatening conditions, they may develop an emotional connection with their captors as a survival strategy. This connection helps them endure the overwhelming psychological distress and fear associated with captivity. By forming this bond, they create a psychological buffer against the harsh realities of their situation. It allows them to focus on the perceived positive aspects of their captors and their environment, which can be crucial for emotional well-being and survival in captivity.

A profound sense of dependency and isolation constitutes potent catalysts for the development of Stockholm Syndrome. When victims find themselves entirely reliant on their captors for fundamental needs like sustenance, water, or protection, it creates a psychological environment conducive to the formation of emotional bonds as a survival strategy. The captors' control over these essential resources plays a crucial role in reinforcing the victims' perception of dependence. By monopolizing access to vital provisions, captors wield a significant influence over the victims' well-being, establishing themselves as the sole source of necessities. This dynamic sets the stage for a complex psychological process wherein captors become not only providers of basic needs but also perceived guardians against potential harm. In this context, emotional dependency develops as a coping mechanism, as victims internalize the belief that aligning themselves with their captors is imperative for their own survival. The victims may begin to see their captors as the arbiters of safety and sustenance, fostering a distorted sense of loyalty and connection.

The emotional bonds forged under such circumstances serve as a means for victims to mitigate feelings of helplessness and fear. The strategy of aligning with captors becomes a psychological defense mechanism against the harsh reality of captivity. By forming an emotional connection, victims may find a semblance of control in an otherwise uncontrollable and threatening environment. This adaptive response, although counterintuitive from an external perspective, can be understood as a survival instinct in the face of overwhelming adversity. The development of Stockholm Syndrome in situations of captivity is intricately linked to the manipulation of basic needs and the psychological perception of dependence. The captors' strategic control over essential resources creates a complex interplay of power dynamics, fostering an environment where emotional bonds with captors become a perceived necessity for the victims' own survival and psychological well-being.

Fear and intimidation play a significant role in the development of Stockholm Syndrome. Perpetrators often employ tactics such as threats, violence, and manipulation to control their victims. Victims may develop Stockholm Syndrome as a means to reduce perceived threats. The captors' ability to instill fear in their victims can create a sense of hopelessness and vulnerability. In response, victims may seek to reduce the threat of violence or harm by aligning themselves with their captors and attempting to gain their favor. This coping strategy is an attempt to mitigate the captors' hostile behavior, reduce their own fear, and establish a sense of control in an otherwise uncontrollable environment.

In some instances, captors may perform small acts of kindness toward their hostages or victims, such as providing food, allowing limited freedom, or demonstrating a degree of compassion. These gestures, while often superficial, can have a profound impact on the development of Stockholm Syndrome. Victims, starved for positive interactions, may interpret these acts as genuine care and concern. They may seize upon these moments as evidence that their captors are not entirely cruel or malevolent. Such acts of kindness create a psychological connection that contrasts with the general atmosphere of hostility and captivity, leading victims to focus on these positive interactions and forming an emotional bond as a result.

The psychological mechanisms triggering Stockholm Syndrome are often rooted in survival strategies. Victims faced with captivity or hostage situations employ these mechanisms as a means of psychological self-preservation. Forming an emotional bond with their captors allows them to reduce the perceived threat, minimize the intensity of fear, and establish some sense of control over their environment. This emotional connection serves as a protective psychological shield, enabling victims to endure their situation. In essence, Stockholm Syndrome represents a complex interplay between fear, dependency, and psychological survival mechanisms. All of which may contribute to this psychological phenomenon.

Cognitive dissonance and Stockholm Syndrome, while distinct psychological concepts, weave a complex tapestry when it comes to comprehending how people cope with conflicting beliefs, attitudes, and emotions, especially within the crucible of high-stress situations. Leon Festinger's cognitive dissonance theory, originating in 1957, provides insight into the discomfort stemming from inconsistent cognitions, wherein they experience mental strain when holding conflicting ideas simultaneously. In contrast, Stockholm Syndrome is characterized by captives developing a peculiar emotional bond with their captors, seemingly paradoxical given the coercive and often harmful circumstances. At a closer look, the relationship between these two psychological phenomena unveils the intricate processes that unfold when they grapple with the dissonance of conflicting emotions and thoughts in the harrowing context of captivity. Cognitive dissonance theory suggests that people strive for internal consistency and will experience psychological discomfort when faced with incongruent beliefs or attitudes. In a hostage or captive situation, this dissonance may arise as victims hold opposing views about their captors – perceiving them as both threats and, paradoxically, as sources of safety or protection.

In theory, cognitive dissonance is the notion that humans are inherently driven to reduce the discomfort resulting from inconsistencies between their beliefs, attitudes, behaviors, and reality. This psychological phenomenon occurs when people hold two or more contradictory cognitions and experience a state of tension as a result.

Cognitive dissonance compels them to seek resolution, prompting them to change their beliefs, attitudes, or actions until they are harmonious and in alignment with one another. If allowed to serve its purpose, it can be a fundamental mechanism for achieving cognitive consistency.

The psychological mechanisms that trigger cognitive dissonance are often at the heart of the emotional bonds that captives develop with their captors. In hostage situations, particularly those involving prolonged captivity or isolation, captors often wield tactics that evoke fear, intimidation, and psychological manipulation. These tactics are employed to control their victims, who, in turn, experience intense emotional distress and fear. In this context, captives may employ cognitive dissonance as a means of coping with the overwhelming psychological distress. By altering their beliefs and attitudes to align with the captors' perspective or by minimizing the threat their captors pose, hostages strive to reduce the dissonance and mitigate their fear. They may begin to rationalize their captors' actions, convincing themselves that their captors are not as malevolent as they initially perceived, even though the evidence points to the contrary. This psychological strategy serves as a defense mechanism, reducing the perceived threat of their captors and providing a semblance of emotional security.

Dependency and isolation are also pivotal factors in the correlation between cognitive dissonance and Stockholm Syndrome. When captives perceive themselves as entirely dependent on their captors for basic necessities such as food, water, or protection, the sense of reliance intensifies the dissonance. Captors often exercise control over access to these vital resources, reinforcing the emotional dependency captives feel. The captors become the sole source of sustenance and safety, making the captives believe that aligning themselves with their captors is the only way to ensure their survival.

Willie Lynch/Stockholm Syndrome compared

Stockholm Syndrome has significant implications for society, criminology, and victim psychology. It forces us to question the intricate relationship between victim and perpetrator, challenging traditional notions of blame and responsibility. The phenomenon also underscores the importance of understanding the psychological mechanisms at play in abusive situations. Stockholm Syndrome refers to the psychological response in which hostages or victims of abduction develop positive feelings or even loyalty toward their captors, while Willie Lynch Syndrome is a concept rooted in a purported historical letter that outlines a strategy for maintaining control and division among enslaved Africans in the United States. These two terms have different origins and contexts, and it is important to note that "Willie Lynch Syndrome" is often regarded as a myth rather than a historical reality. Nonetheless, there are some common threads between these concepts in terms of power dynamics, psychological manipulation, and the enduring effects of historical trauma. If we were to closely compare Stockholm Syndrome and Willie Lynch Syndrome, all we have to do is replace the captor with the word master. At first glance, the common thread here is the human capacity to adapt to extreme circumstances by employing psychological coping mechanisms. In both situations, individuals find ways to endure their realities, whether it is in a hostage situation or within the context of historical oppression. We can also find, at first glance, one uncommon thread in both disorders, Stockholm Syndrome does not perpetuate itself generationally, at least as far as we know.

One common thread between Stockholm Syndrome and Willie Lynch Syndrome is the exploration of power dynamics and psychological manipulation. In Stockholm Syndrome, the power dynamic is evident in the captor-hostage relationship. Hostages, often in a vulnerable and powerless position, may develop positive feelings or a sense of loyalty toward their captors as a means of coping with their situation. The captors, in this context, hold the power and control over the hostages' well-being, which can create a sense of dependency and emotional attachment. In the case of Willie Lynch Syndrome, the concept involves the manipulation of power dynamics within a system of oppression. The letter attributed to Willie Lynch outlines strategies for maintaining control over enslaved Africans by creating divisions and hierarchies among them. This involves psychological manipulation to pit slaves against each other, creating a sense of powerlessness and dependence on the oppressors. Both concepts highlight how inherent power imbalances and psychological manipulation can lead to a few individuals or groups forming bonds or loyalties with those in positions of authority or control. This dynamic reflects the impact of power differentials on human behavior and relationships.

Another common thread is the role of psychological coping mechanisms in both Stockholm Syndrome and discussions of Willie Lynch Syndrome. In the case of Stockholm Syndrome, developing a bond with captors is often seen as a coping mechanism in response to extreme stress, isolation, and captivity. Hostages may engage in this emotional attachment as a survival strategy to reduce perceived threats and navigate their traumatic circumstances. The Willie Lynch Syndrome also touches on coping mechanisms. It suggests that enslaved Africans were subjected to psychological and physical trauma as a means of control. The concept implies that some enslaved individuals might have developed coping mechanisms, such as internalizing a sense of inferiority or internal divisions, as a way to survive within an oppressive system.

Emotional bonds and attachment play a significant role in both Stockholm Syndrome and Willie Lynch Syndrome. In Stockholm

Syndrome, hostages may form emotional bonds with their captors as a way to cope with the emotional and physical trauma they experience. These bonds can lead to empathy and even loyalty toward the captors. In discussions of Willie Lynch Syndrome, the concept implies that enslaved Africans might have developed emotional attachments, not to their oppressors, but to the system of oppression itself. This attachment could manifest in internalized beliefs or behaviors that perpetuated divisions and hierarchies among enslaved individuals. The common thread is the human capacity for forming emotional bonds and attachments, even in situations of extreme duress or oppression. These emotional connections can shape their perceptions, beliefs, and behaviors. This can be encapsulated in the period following the emancipation of those enslaved in the United States. Some former slaves returned to their masters. The years following the American Civil War and the Emancipation Proclamation of 1863 were characterized by profound changes and uncertainty. Formerly enslaved African Americans, now free individuals, faced a daunting and often overwhelming transition from lives marked by bondage to the uncertain prospect of freedom. It is noteworthy that not all former slaves who returned to their former masters did so willingly or out of a sense of loyalty. In some cases, they were forced or coerced to return, facing the threat of violence or economic destitution if they refused. The power dynamics and lingering social structures of the pre-emancipation South were not easily dismantled, and some of them found themselves trapped in situations where their choices were severely limited.

Both Stockholm Syndrome and Willie Lynch Syndrome also highlight the enduring effects of trauma. In the case of Stockholm Syndrome, the trauma of captivity and the emotional bonds formed with captors can have lasting psychological impacts on hostages. Even after their release, some may continue to defend or empathize with their captors. In discussions of Willie Lynch Syndrome, the concept suggests that the trauma and division imposed on enslaved Africans had enduring effects on subsequent generations. It implies that the legacy of this trauma may have contributed to ongoing divisions within African American communities and the internalization of oppressive beliefs and behaviors. The common thread is the recognition that trauma, whether experienced in a hostage situation or through historical oppression, can have long-lasting psychological, social, and cultural impacts. It underscores the importance of acknowledging and addressing the effects of trauma on individuals and communities.

Stockholm Syndrome and Willie Lynch Syndrome underscore the complexity of human behavior and the multifaceted nature of human responses to adversity. In the case of Stockholm Syndrome, the development of positive feelings or loyalties toward captors is a complex and often counterintuitive response to a traumatic situation. It challenges traditional notions of victimhood and resistance. In discussions of Willie Lynch Syndrome, the concept, while disputed and controversial, highlights the intricate ways in which people and communities may respond to systemic oppression. It acknowledges the complexity of the human experience within a historical context marked by profound injustices. The common thread is the recognition that human behavior is not easily categorized or explained. Both concepts invite us to delve into the intricate and sometimes paradoxical ways in which individuals and communities navigate situations of power, trauma, and adversity.

Perhaps what makes Willie Lynch Syndrome and Stockholm Syndrome most alike is the cognitive dissonance that both seem to cause in their victims, at least in the beginning stages of capitulation. It would seem commonsensical to assume that at some stage before conforming, people would have conflicting ideas or beliefs from their own. At this point, they would feel unease or extreme tension in their attempt to rationalize their situation. Whether it be a hostage scenario or enslavement, that mental turmoil has to be relieved. For submission to happen, several steps have to be undertaken to rationalize the ultimate decision to submit.

The convergence of Willie Lynch Syndrome and Stockholm Syndrome can be attributed, in part, to the deep-rooted survival instincts inherent when facing oppressive circumstances. The parallel lies in the victims' reliance on the perceived benevolence of their captors for survival. In the context of Willie Lynch Syndrome, a term associated with the purported methods used to control slaves, those subjected to this form of oppression found themselves dependent on the perceived generosities of their masters. This dependency, driven by a survival instinct, compelled slaves to navigate a delicate balance, as they often had to rely on the mercy of those in power for their basic needs such as food, shelter, and safety.

A common thread between both syndromes is the profound impact on major institutions. Victims of Willie Lynch Syndrome, particularly slaves, were often subjected to systematic efforts aimed at dismantling familial and communal bonds, disrupting cultural institutions, and eroding social structures. This destruction was calculated to reinforce the dominance of the oppressors. Similarly, in cases of Stockholm Syndrome, captives may experience the utter destruction of their sense of normalcy and security, as captors exert control not only over physical freedom but also over psychological well-being. The survival instinct emerges as a unifying element, driving those in both scenarios to adapt to their circumstances in ways that may seem counterintuitive. The dependency on perceived acts of generosity from those in power becomes a means of securing survival, albeit within the confines of an oppressive environment. By acknowledging the role of survival instincts in these syndromes, a deeper understanding of the complex interplay between power dynamics, dependence, and psychological responses in situations of oppression and captivity emerges. These insights contribute to a more comprehensive grasp of the human experience in the face of adversity, shedding light on the intricate ways they navigate and survive in challenging environments.

The Physiological Aspects

The physiological aspects of Willie Lynch Syndrome and Stockholm Syndrome represent two distinct but interconnected psychological phenomena that shed light on the profound and lasting impacts of extreme psychological manipulation, control, and subjugation. While these phenomena originate in different historical contexts, they share common threads in terms of the physiological responses they elicit. In this exploration, we will delve into the physiological aspects that connect these two phenomena, emphasizing the roles of stress, coping mechanisms, and emotional attachment in understanding their enduring effects on individuals and communities.

Both Willie Lynch Syndrome and Stockholm Syndrome are characterized by the imposition of extreme stress and psychological manipulation. In the context of Willie Lynch Syndrome, enslaved individuals were subjected to relentless physical labor, harsh living conditions, and the constant threat of violence. This exposure to extreme stress triggered physiological responses in the body, primarily involving the release of stress hormones such as cortisol and adrenaline. In situations where hostages or captives experience Stockholm Syndrome, they also endure prolonged stress and fear during their captivity. The threat to their physical and emotional well-being results in the release of stress hormones as part of the body's natural "fight-or-flight" response. This physiological reaction heightens vigilance and alertness, preparing the individual to confront or escape from the perceived threat. The common thread here is the role of stress in triggering physiological responses that shape their emotional and psychological experiences. Stress, whether experienced by enslaved individuals or hostages, creates a state of heightened arousal that influences how they perceive their circumstances and the people controlling them.

Those subjected to the stress and manipulation associated with both Willie Lynch Syndrome and Stockholm Syndrome often develop coping mechanisms as a means of adapting to their circumstances. These coping mechanisms, which serve as both psychological and physiological responses to extreme stress, aim to reduce feelings of fear, helplessness, and anxiety. In the context of Willie Lynch Syndrome, enslaved individuals may have developed coping mechanisms such as submission, compliance, or the suppression of resistance as a means of self-preservation. These coping strategies were adaptive in the context of slavery, as they reduced the risk of physical harm or retribution. Physiologically, this adaptation involved the suppression of emotional responses and the activation of the body's stress response for survival. Similarly, in cases of Stockholm Syndrome, hostages may develop coping mechanisms to manage their fear and anxiety. These mechanisms can include identifying with their captors, empathizing with them, and forming emotional attachments as a means of seeking safety and security. The physiological aspect of these coping mechanisms often involves the release of hormones like oxytocin, which fosters emotional bonding and attachment, even in the context of captivity. The common thread here is the role of coping mechanisms as adaptive responses to extreme stress and manipulation. These mechanisms may lead to the development of emotional attachments that are rooted in the physiological responses to stress, effectively blurring the lines between captor and captive.

Willie Lynch Syndrome and Stockholm Syndrome both involve the development of emotional attachments between people in situations characterized by unequal power dynamics. In the context of Willie Lynch Syndrome, the emotional attachment may manifest as a form of loyalty or dependence on the part of the enslaved toward their oppressors. The emotional bonds created under these circumstances may be rooted in the physiological responses to stress, such as the release of stress hormones that influence emotional and cognitive processes. In Stockholm Syndrome, hostages develop emotional attachments towards their captors, which can be a survival mechanism in situations where captives perceive their captors as both sources of danger and protection. The physiological aspect of this attachment is linked to the release of hormones like oxytocin, which fosters trust, empathy, and emotional bonding. The common thread here is the presence of emotional attachment in situations of extreme stress and manipulation. In both Willie Lynch Syndrome and Stockholm Syndrome, the physiological responses to stress, coupled with the development of coping mechanisms, contribute to the formation of emotional bonds that can endure even after the immediate threat has been removed.

Both Willie Lynch Syndrome and Stockholm Syndrome can have long-term psychological effects on those who have experienced these phenomena. The physiological responses, coping mechanisms, and emotional attachments developed during these situations can persist even after the removal of the immediate threat. In the case of Willie Lynch Syndrome, the long-term effects may manifest as a complex interplay between submission, compliance, and resistance in the face of ongoing systemic oppression. The physiological aspect of these effects may include heightened stress reactivity, altered emotional regulation, and the internalization of feelings of powerlessness. For those who have experienced Stockholm Syndrome, the long-term effects may involve enduring emotional attachments or a sense of loyalty to former captors. Physiologically, the emotional bonds formed during captivity can continue to influence a person's behavior and decision-making, even when they are no longer in immediate danger. The common thread is the lasting impact of the physiological responses, coping mechanisms, and emotional attachments that were initially developed as survival strategies. These enduring effects can influence a person's perception of their own agency, relationships, and sense of self, reinforcing the profound and lasting influence of these phenomena.

A significant commonality between Willie Lynch Syndrome and Stockholm Syndrome lies in the broader social dynamics and blatant oppression that are the foundation of both phenomena. Willie Lynch Syndrome, as a set of tactics used to maintain control over enslaved African Americans, was part of a broader system of racial oppression and dehumanization. Similarly, Stockholm Syndrome often occurs in situations where captors hold power and control over their victims. The captives, who are subjected to fear and manipulation, develop emotional attachments that serve as a survival mechanism within the confines of that power dynamic. The common thread here is the role of power imbalances and systemic oppression in fostering situations where physiological responses to stress, coping mechanisms, and emotional attachments become prominent. Both Willie Lynch Syndrome and Stockholm Syndrome are rooted in power structures that perpetuate the subjugation of one group by another, whether through slavery or captivity.

The Physiological Aspect of Slave Mentality

The notion of the "slave mentality" encompasses profound historical and physiological dimensions, offering crucial insights into the enduring repercussions of slavery on individuals and their descendants. The institution of slavery, with its pervasive and dehumanizing nature, went beyond inflicting physical and psychological abuse; it also etched a lasting imprint on the physiological well-being of those subjected to its brutality. A comprehensive examination of the physiological aspects of the slave mentality is indispensable for unraveling the intricate ways in which slavery shaped the health and biology of enslaved populations, and understanding how these effects persist across subsequent generations.

The physiological aspect of the slave mentality is a complex and multifaceted dimension of the legacy of slavery. It encompasses the physical toll that the institution of slavery exacted on the enslaved and how these effects continue to manifest in the descendants of enslaved populations. To comprehensively understand this aspect, it is essential to explore various elements, including the physical abuse endured by slaves, the nutritional deprivations they faced, and the intergenerational transmission of physiological changes resulting from the slave experience. The enslaved endured strenuous labor, grueling working conditions, and often brutal treatment at the hands of their masters. These physical hardships took a severe toll on their bodies. Backbreaking labor in fields, mines, or domestic settings led to chronic musculoskeletal issues and injuries. The physical demands of slavery resulted in high rates of chronic pain, arthritis, and physical disabilities among the enslaved population. Furthermore, the constant threat of violence, including whippings, beatings, and other forms of punishment, left lasting physical scars and traumatic injuries. These traumatic experiences contributed to long-term health issues and psychological trauma. The physical abuse endured by them was a harsh and brutal aspect of the slave mentality.

The physiological aspect of the slave mentality is intrinsically linked to the psychological stress and trauma endured by them. The constant threat of violence, the complete lack of personal autonomy, and the harsh living conditions subjected slaves to significant psychological stress. This stress, in turn, had profound physiological effects on their bodies. Chronic stress triggers a physiological response that includes the release of stress hormones such as cortisol. Elevated and sustained levels of cortisol can have detrimental effects on various bodily systems. For the enslaved, these effects could manifest in increased susceptibility to various illnesses, including cardiovascular diseases, hypertension, and compromised immune function. Moreover, the intergenerational transmission of stress is a key aspect of the physiological legacy of slavery. Studies have shown that the descendants of enslaved individuals may inherit certain physiological responses to stress, which can increase their vulnerability to stress-related health issues. This intergenerational transmission of stress is part of the broader physiological inheritance of the slave mentality.

One of the most compelling aspects of the physiological legacy of the slave mentality is the concept of epigenetic inheritance. Epigenetics refers to changes in gene expression that occur without alterations to the underlying DNA sequence. These changes can be influenced by environmental factors, including experiences of trauma and stress. Recent research has shed light on the epigenetic changes that may be associated with the descendants of enslaved individuals. These changes can influence gene expression and impact their susceptibility to various health conditions. While epigenetic inheritance is a complex and evolving field of study, it provides a compelling framework for understanding how the physiological aspects of the slave mentality can be transmitted across generations.

The enslaved developed various coping mechanisms to endure the physical and psychological hardships of slavery. These coping strategies could have both positive and negative effects on their health. For example, some of them turned to herbal remedies and traditional healing practices to address their health issues. These practices, passed down through generations, continue to influence the health behaviors of African American communities today. However, coping mechanisms also included behaviors such as overeating, smoking, and substance use as ways to manage stress and trauma. These maladaptive coping strategies have contributed to health disparities and negative health outcomes among African Americans, further connecting the historical experiences of slavery to contemporary health challenges.

Healthcare disparities are a critical component of the physiological aspect of the slave mentality. The enslaved had limited access to medical care and were often subjected to substandard or exploitative medical practices. This historical legacy of medical mistreatment and discrimination has had a lasting impact on the healthcare experiences of African Americans. The Tuskegee Syphilis Study, for instance, is a well-known example of medical exploitation and abuse. The unethical study, conducted by the United States Public Health Service, left a legacy of mistrust and skepticism toward the medical establishment within African American communities. This mistrust has contributed to healthcare disparities, including delayed diagnoses and reduced access to quality care, which continue to affect the health of African Americans today.

The physiological aspect of the slave mentality in modern society encompasses a range of complex and interconnected dimensions, including health disparities, stress-related conditions, nutrition, epigenetic inheritance, coping mechanisms, and healthcare disparities. It reflects the enduring impact of historical slavery on the health and well-being of African Americans. Understanding and addressing the physiological consequences of the slave mentality is a critical step toward achieving health equity and rectifying the historical injustices. Recognizing the interplay between physiological responses and social determinants of health is essential to dismantling the enduring effects of the slave mentality in contemporary society. Recognizing the physiological aspects of the slave mentality in modern societies is a critical step toward understanding its correlation to victim mentality.

When examining the physiological aspect of Stockholm Syndrome, it is crucial to understand the body's response to stress. The stress response, often referred to as the "fight or flight" response, is an ancient and adaptive mechanism that has evolved to protect people from immediate danger. When faced with a perceived threat, the body releases stress hormones, primarily cortisol and adrenaline. These hormones trigger a cascade of physiological changes designed to prepare them to either fight or flight. The release of cortisol and adrenaline results in increased heart rate, heightened alertness, and mobilization of energy reserves. Blood is shunted away from non-essential functions, such as digestion, towards vital organs and muscles. This physiological response is intended to provide them with the physical and mental resources needed to survive in a threatening situation. In the context of Stockholm Syndrome, it is this very stress response that plays a significant role. Hostages or victims of abduction are subjected to prolonged and extreme stress, often in life-threatening situations. Their bodies respond to this stress by releasing stress hormones, resulting in heightened vigilance and increased alertness. This physiological response, designed for survival, can have profound effects on an individual's perception of their captors.

While the stress response is designed for immediate survival, it can also contribute to a complex bonding mechanism in situations like Stockholm Syndrome. As the body releases stress hormones, these chemicals can influence a person's emotional state and decision-making. The heightened vigilance and alertness associated with the stress response can lead to an intensified focus on the captor, who becomes a central figure in the victim's life during the period of captivity. In essence, the physiological response to stress can lead to an emotional attachment to the captor as a means of seeking safety and security. This attachment can be reinforced by the captor's behavior, which may include occasional acts of kindness or apparent concern for the victim's well-being. In response to these actions, the victim may perceive the captor as a source of both danger and protection, leading to conflicting feelings.

The physiological aspects of Stockholm Syndrome are closely related to the biology of attachment. Attachment is a fundamental aspect of human behavior, and it plays a crucial role in the formation of social bonds and relationships. This biological basis of attachment can be hijacked in situations of captivity and hostage-taking, leading to the development of Stockholm Syndrome. In the context of Stockholm Syndrome, the captor's occasional acts of kindness or apparent concern for the victim can trigger the release of oxytocin. This hormone, released in response to these positive interactions, can foster a sense of attachment and emotional connection to the captor. The victim may perceive the captor as a source of emotional support and comfort, despite the inherently threatening nature of the situation.

Cognitive dissonance, a psychological phenomenon involving the discomfort arising from holding conflicting beliefs or attitudes, is not confined to the realm of the mind alone; it also manifests physiological changes within the body. The intricate interplay between cognition and physiology becomes evident as cognitive dissonance triggers alterations in stress hormone levels and neurotransmitter activity in the brain. This physiological response underscores the profound impact that conflicting thoughts and emotions can have on the body. Those grappling with cognitive dissonance may find themselves compelled to reconcile the incongruity between perceiving their captors as threats and simultaneously seeking an emotional connection with them. In an effort to mitigate this internal conflict, they may engage in a cognitive reinterpretation of their captors' actions, framing them as acts of kindness or concern. This cognitive reframing serves as a psychological coping mechanism, aimed at reducing the dissonance between the perceived threat and the desire for attachment.

The physiological aspect of this process is particularly intriguing. The reinterpretation of captors' actions as benevolent can trigger the release of hormones such as oxytocin within the brain. Oxytocin, often referred to as the "bonding hormone" or "love hormone," plays a crucial role in fostering feelings of attachment, trust, and emotional bonding. The release of oxytocin, in response to the cognitive reinterpretation, contributes to the establishment of a psychological bond between captor and captive. This physiological response is a key element in the development of Stockholm Syndrome.

The reinforcing nature of this physiological response further complicates the emotional dynamics of Stockholm Syndrome. As oxytocin levels rise in response to the cognitive reconciliation, some people may experience an intensification of emotional attachment to their captors. This paradoxical connection, born out of a complex interplay between cognition and physiology, deepens the psychological entanglement between captors and captives.

Furthermore, Stockholm Syndrome is also influenced by the increased alertness experienced by hostages or victims of abduction. Prolonged exposure to a perceived threat and constant vigilance can have profound effects on a person's physiology. The continuous release of stress hormones, such as cortisol and adrenaline, can result in heightened alertness and a state of chronic stress. In this state of hypervigilance, they may become hyper-focused on their captors, monitoring their every move and gesture for signs of danger or safety. This intense focus can intensify the emotional attachment to the captor, as the captor becomes the central figure in the victim's life during captivity. The physiological consequences of hypervigilance can reinforce the emotional bond and the development of Stockholm Syndrome.

The Triggers

One of the primary triggers of the slave mentality in modern society is the historical legacy of slavery and the collective memory of its horrors. Slavery, which persisted worldwide for centuries, was marked by the brutal subjugation and dehumanization of its victims. The trauma experienced by enslaved individuals and their descendants left an indelible mark on the collective memory of all affected communities. The history of slavery is passed down through generations, often through oral traditions, historical accounts, and cultural expressions. The stories of resilience, suffering, and resistance serve as a constant reminder of the historical trauma endured by slaves. This collective memory triggers a range of emotions, including anger, grief, and a sense of injustice, which can evoke the slave mentality. The historical legacy of slavery also perpetuates the intergenerational transmission of trauma. Descendants of the enslaved inherit not only the stories of their ancestors but also the emotional and psychological scars of their traumatic experiences. This transmission of historical trauma triggers the slave mentality in modern society, manifesting as emotional pain, mistrust, and a deep sense of historical injustice.

The victims of Willie Lynch Syndrome, particularly the descendants of slaves, often find themselves entrenched in an environment that perpetuates and reinforces the conditions outlined by this historical concept. One striking aspect of this environment is the pervasive perception of constant threat, particularly in the context of interactions with law enforcement. The fear of police encounters, often fueled by historical and contemporary systemic issues, becomes a palpable and persistent reality for many people. This sustained perception of threat contributes to a heightened state of vigilance, further ingraining the psychological aspects of Willie Lynch Syndrome.

Another facet of this reinforcing environment is the existence of small acts of kindness or concessions from those who may be perceived as assailants. This can be likened to government assistance programs or handouts, which, while providing some relief or support, come from a system that may be inherently oppressive. The duality of these actions, where assistance is granted alongside the perpetuation of inequalities, creates a complex dynamic that reinforces a sense of dependency and, in turn, aligns with the manipulative strategies outlined in the Willie Lynch narrative.

Isolation, a key aspect prescribed by Willie Lynch, continues to be a triggering condition in the contemporary context. Those who feel isolated from their communities or are subject to societal marginalization may internalize a sense of helplessness and dependency on the very structures that contribute to their isolation. We can see this manifestation in the modern housing projects which can be interpreted as being isolated from the rest of society. This isolation can be exhibited not only physically but also socially and economically, further perpetuating a cycle of vulnerability and reinforcing the psychological aspects of Willie Lynch Syndrome. The pervasive belief that there are no viable solutions with positive outcomes becomes a potent psychological barrier. The notion that systemic change is unattainable or that personal agency is limited can lead to a sense of resignation. This fatalistic perspective serves as the final nail in the coffin, so to speak, cementing the mindset that resists empowerment or proactive efforts to break free from the conditions associated with Willie Lynch Syndrome.

The perception of systemic racial discrimination, inequality, and inequities are persistent and pervasive triggers of the slave mentality in contemporary society. Despite legal advancements and the civil rights movements, the idea of structural racism, systemic discrimination, and unequal outcomes continue to affect the lives of modern society. Racial disparities in education, employment, housing, and criminal justice are perceived tangible manifestations of this ongoing discrimination. The perception of racial discrimination triggers the slave mentality by reinforcing the sense of being marginalized, oppressed, and devalued. Those who believe to have faced racial discrimination may internalize negative stereotypes and biases, which can erode their self-esteem and sense of agency. This internalization of racism is a form of psychological oppression that harkens back to the dehumanization endured by enslaved individuals. Racial discrimination also triggers a sense of vulnerability and hypervigilance. Marginalized racial and ethnic groups often live with the constant awareness of the potential for bias, microaggressions, or overt racism. This heightened vigilance, driven by the fear of discrimination or violence, is a manifestation of the psychological impact of the slave mentality. It underscores the enduring consequences of historical oppression and the deep-rooted triggers that persist in modern society.

Criminal justice disparities and over-policing are triggers of the slave mentality that have garnered significant attention in recent years. African Americans are reportedly disproportionately affected by over-policing, racial profiling, and harsher sentencing. This perception of systemic discrimination contributes to a sense of vulnerability, injustice, and a lack of trust in the criminal justice system. The experience of criminal justice disparities triggers the slave mentality by reinforcing the perception of African Americans as inherently criminal or dangerous. People who face over-policing may internalize a sense of guilt or undesirability, reminiscent of the historical criminalization of African Americans during slavery. This internalized stigma affects their self-esteem and psychological well-being. Over-policing also evokes a sense of constant surveillance and hypervigilance. African Americans, particularly young men, often live with the fear of racial profiling and police violence. The police are just the most obvious example. Willie Lynch needed the slaves to distrust each other and only trust in their masters. Slaves were made to turn on each other. They became, perceivably, a greater threat to each other than their master. The comfort of a family unit was also destroyed leaving no support mechanisms to find hope. In comes the master again! By offering small acts of kindness, like food, water, and comforting words after killing the strong males, he gives hope that some will survive. The government that offers free stuff is the same government that oversees the police. The police who instill fear and are perceived as a threat. This heightened vigilance is a manifestation of the psychological triggers associated with the slave mentality, reflecting the historical trauma of surveillance and control.

Educational disparities and limited opportunities are additional triggers of the slave mentality in modern society. Unequal access to quality education and opportunities for advancement is a pressing issue for many marginalized communities. Disparities in educational resources, curriculum quality, and access to advanced courses contribute to unequal educational outcomes. The experience of educational disparities triggers the slave mentality by perpetuating a sense of limited potential and diminished self-worth. People who face limited educational opportunities may internalize a sense of intellectual inferiority, reminiscent of the historical denial of education to enslaved individuals. This internalized sense of inadequacy hampers their aspirations and self-esteem. Limited opportunities also evoke a sense of restricted agency and social mobility. The lack of access to quality education and opportunities for advancement reinforces a cycle of disadvantage and economic hardship. This cycle perpetuates the psychological triggers associated with the slave mentality, including dependency and a lack of empowerment.

Isolation is a prevalent and powerful factor that contributes to the modern manifestation of the "slave mentality," a term that metaphorically describes the enduring psychological and emotional impacts of historical slavery on marginalized communities. While the institution of slavery has formally ended, its legacy continues to exert profound influence in contemporary society. Isolation, whether imposed or self-imposed, serves as a trigger for the perpetuation of the psychological and emotional aspects of the slave mentality. In this exploration, we delve into the connections between isolation and the modern slave mentality, illuminating how social, economic, and systemic factors conspire to maintain these enduring effects. When I think about the isolation, I think about the inner cities of metropolises like Chicago or Baltimore. The poor are zoned off from the middle class and the rich by an invisible barrier. These areas are plagued with failed programs and policies that lead to a poor education structure, the total lack of decent paying jobs, and are run down to the level of dilapidation that can only be comparable to the slums of some third-world countries. These circumstances perpetuate the isolation by choking out any means of creating opportunities to excel, the means to find hope were also relinquished.

Social isolation is a powerful driver of the modern slave mentality, particularly among marginalized communities, including African Americans and other minority groups. The enduring consequences of slavery have left deep-seated social divisions and racial hierarchies that continue to affect individuals and communities. These divisions, often perpetuated by systemic racism and discrimination, contribute to the social isolation of marginalized groups. Those who experience social isolation may internalize a sense of marginalization and exclusion. This internalized feeling of being an outsider, perpetuated by a society that has not fully dismantled systemic racism, triggers the slave mentality by reinforcing a perception of inferiority and unworthiness. Social isolation exacerbates a sense of powerlessness and a lack of agency, characteristics reminiscent of the historical experiences of enslaved people. Furthermore, social isolation can lead to the formation of insular communities that are disconnected from broader societal opportunities. This isolation perpetuates a sense of dependency and limited access to resources and opportunities, evoking the psychological triggers of the slave mentality. The impact of social isolation is compounded by the intersections of race, class, and socioeconomic status, which create complex barriers to social inclusion.

Economic isolation, closely intertwined with social isolation, is another potent trigger for the modern slave mentality. Economic disparities and limited opportunities disproportionately affect marginalized communities. The enduring effects of historical slavery, compounded by systemic discrimination and economic injustice, result in restricted access to economic resources and opportunities for advancement. Those who experience economic isolation may internalize a sense of powerlessness and dependency. The limited access to economic resources and opportunities reinforces a cycle of disadvantage, reminiscent of the economic exploitation experienced by enslaved individuals. This internalized sense of economic inferiority triggers the slave mentality, leading to diminished self-esteem and aspirations. Economic isolation is compounded by the lack of access to quality education and opportunities for advancement. The resulting limited social mobility perpetuates a sense of restricted agency, harkening back to the historical denial of educational and economic opportunities to enslaved people. This combination of economic and educational isolation reinforces the psychological triggers associated with the slave mentality, including a lack of empowerment and potential.

Final Thoughts

After prolonged exposure to these environments, it is only understandable that even the strongest mind will concede. At some point, it would appear that there is no way out or that there are no solutions. Being constantly exposed to these triggers, a person can only learn to adapt. That adaptation, over time, becomes one's state of normality. So normal that it becomes extremely difficult if even at all possible, to free oneself from the disparities.

It's incredible that both psychological conditions produce the same physiological symptoms. These symptoms cause an identical mental condition by which the attempt is made to achieve cognitive constancy; to be alleviated from cognitive dissonance. The captor or master perceives and treats the victim or slave as inferior. The oppressor methodically presents a false conception of reality at the same time they are both positively and negatively reinforcing their false narratives until the oppressed, for what is perceived as an act of self-preservation, develop and new behavior that they cannot distinguish from reality and the false narratives that are now accepted as true and normal.

The common threads that connect the physiological aspects of Willie Lynch Syndrome and Stockholm Syndrome revolve around stress, coping mechanisms, emotional attachment, long-term psychological effects, and the influence of broader social dynamics and systemic oppression. Despite their different historical and contemporary contexts, these phenomena reveal the intricate relationship between the mind and body when confronted with extreme stress and psychological manipulation. Understanding these common threads is essential in recognizing the enduring impact of these experiences on individuals and communities and addressing the broader issues of power, control, and resilience. In retrospect, though both the Willie

Lynch and the Stockholm syndromes are very similar in their definitions, the criteria or circumstances needed to be created for them to evoke a new behavior, the psychological and physiological causations and ramifications, and the havoc they bring to the lives of the oppressed victims. Stockholm Syndrome usually ends with the separation of the hostage from the captor. Willie Lynch Syndrome, on the other hand, was designed to perpetuate itself throughout generations. The true slave, or victim, does not necessarily need to be shackled, assaulted, or manipulated in any way to comply.

Chapter Three: The Philosophy of Subordination

Subordination

Aristotle wrote, "That which can foresee by the exercise of mind is by nature intended to be lord and master, and that which can with its body give effect to such foresight is a subject, and by nature a slave." Simplified, this bold statement says people who have the cognitive ability to conceive an idea are, by nature, masters. Those who have the ability to manifest these ideas into a physical reality are by nature, slaves. His somewhat juvenile concept of subordination may be offensive or looked at purely by his vernacular. If, however, one would remove one's emotions from the statement, one would realize that it objectively describes the world we live in today. Instead of masters, we have corporations who are making record profits, while the workers are fighting off poverty. We have governments comprised of rich people but their "constituents" are mostly poor or middle class. In nature, we also find similar hierarchies. Thus, Aristotle was not necessarily wrong in what he found to be very obvious.

Naturally, some people are comfortable with leading others while most people would rather follow. Both coincide with each other but are not mutually exclusive. The boundaries are permeable. A good leader knows when and how to follow. Likewise, a good follower knows when and how to lead. Given, they may only be able to accomplish the other's role for a short time, the possibility does exist. We make these choices about ourselves regularly without batting an eye or giving it a second thought. The positions we apply to are relegated to some form or a combination of these two roles. We can be the skilled worker on the floor in a factory, for example, or we could be the shift manager who also plays the follower role in his management structure.

To understand the correlation between natural subordination and Slave Mentality, we can apply the theory of truth and power, introduced by Michael Foucault which explains the relationship between power and truth either through internal or external validations. He contends that we can, on the one hand, stand witness to how pop-culture influences the perception of the masses of their social, cultural, and economic conditions and the ruling class uses the media to control truths. The incident involving a White policeman accused of choking a Black man with his knee is a prime example of this internal validity. Months before the facts could be determined in a court of law, the ruling class used the media to manipulate society's intended response to trigger discourse with the purpose of justifying people's jaded perception of class structure. In this case, the narrative suggests the poor are oppressed and murdered by the rich through the police. On the other hand, our Republic itself is his example of an external validation. Our "elected" leaders are trusted to exercise the powers given to them by the Constitution. However, legitimizing this power is the constructed truth and so the ruled tolerate subordination since they believe in the truth that the "elected" officials have unprecedented power over them.

If we recall the concepts that Lynch taught and apply them to the explanation for the tolerance of subordination, we see that there are parallels that come to the same conclusion, even if worded differently. The ruled, who can otherwise be described as slaves, perceive themselves as inferior to the ruling class, who can otherwise be described as masters. The masters present a false sense of reality and use the media to make this false reality true. The slaves receive this new reality and accept their social-economic position as tolerable because it fits within the construct of the new truth. Since this is the attempt to achieve cognitive constancy and justify cognitive dissonance, this is consistent with both the Stockholm and Willie Lynch syndromes.

Subordination, on its own, would not suffice in maintaining a status quo indefinitely. In fact, the theory of truth and power suggests that this power structure may eventually not be accepted because it's built on a false consciousness. In this case, the awakening of the slave class will be the catalyst to achieve justice through a revolution or an insurrection. The idea of subordination will need to be coupled with other controlling agents designed to prolong the clutches it clutches.

Authoritarianism

In political and governance contexts, subordination can manifest through authoritarian regimes where leaders hold immense power, and citizens have limited rights or freedoms. Authoritarianism is a form of governance characterized by centralized authority and strict control over society. In authoritarian regimes, power is concentrated in the hands of a single leader, a small group, or a ruling party, often with limited political freedoms and civil liberties for citizens. This system tends to prioritize stability and order over individual rights and democratic principles. Authoritarianism can stifle dissent, limit press freedom, and suppress political opposition. It contrasts with democracy, where power is distributed among elected representatives and citizens enjoy greater political participation. The impact of authoritarianism on a society can vary widely, from stability to repression and human rights abuses.

The institution of slavery itself was a manifestation of authoritarianism where enslaved people were subjected to the absolute authority of slaveholders. The hierarchical structure of slavery, with its rigid power differentials, laid the groundwork for the exercise of authoritarian control. People who were enslaved had no legal rights, were denied autonomy, and were subjected to severe consequences for disobedience. Authoritarianism during slavery extended beyond the individual slaveholder to encompass the broader societal and legal frameworks that upheld the institution. Laws were enacted to maintain control over the enslaved population, further entrenching the authoritarian nature of the system. The use of violence, intimidation, and strict regulations contributed to the establishment of an authoritarian order that stifled dissent and maintained social order.

The psychological dimensions of authoritarianism within the context of slavery are profound and enduring. Those who were enslaved internalized the authority of their oppressors, leading to a slave mentality characterized by submission, compliance, and a diminished sense of self-worth. The authoritarian control exerted by slaveholders was not only physical but also psychological, shaping the mindset of the enslaved population. The internalization of authoritarian values and power dynamics has been passed down through generations, contributing to the persistence of a slave mentality in some communities. This internalized oppression manifests as a belief in the inherent superiority of certain groups and a sense of learned helplessness among those historically subjected to authoritarian rule.

While the formal institution of slavery has been abolished, the echoes of authoritarianism persist in various forms within contemporary society. Structural inequalities, discriminatory practices, and systemic oppression contribute to the perpetuation of authoritarian dynamics that impact marginalized communities. Authoritarianism can be observed in the criminal justice system, where communities of color are disproportionately targeted and subjected to harsher sentences. Policing practices, such as racial profiling and the militarization of law enforcement, reflect authoritarian tendencies that perpetuate a sense of fear and subservience within certain communities. The workplace, too, can be a breeding ground for authoritarianism, with power imbalances and exploitative practices disproportionately affecting vulnerable populations. Economic disparities, lack of workers' rights, and limited access to opportunities mirror the authoritarian structures that characterized the historical institution of slavery. Media and political discourse also play a role in perpetuating authoritarian tendencies. The dissemination of biased information, the scapegoating of marginalized groups, and the suppression of dissenting voices contribute to an environment where authoritarian values persist. The manipulation of narratives, reminiscent of historical attempts to control enslaved populations, continues to shape public opinion and perpetuate a skewed power dynamic.

Authoritarianism, deeply intertwined with the historical institution of slavery, has left enduring imprints on the collective consciousness of marginalized communities. The psychological dimensions of authoritarian control, the historical connections, and contemporary manifestations underscore the complex relationship between authoritarianism and a slave mentality. Breaking free from this legacy necessitates a multifaceted approach that addresses systemic inequalities, promotes education, and actively engages in the dismantling of oppressive structures. By understanding the historical roots and confronting contemporary manifestations, society can work towards a future marked by democracy, equality, and the eradication of the persistent shadows of a slave mentality.

Economic Exploitation

Economic exploitation refers to the unjust and often systemic practice of taking advantage of certain individuals or groups for financial gain or control while offering them limited compensation or benefits. It commonly occurs in industries where vulnerable workers, such as low-wage laborers face harsh working conditions such as low pay and inadequate labor protections. Economic exploitation is designed to perpetuate income and wealth disparities, hinder social upward mobility, and contribute to generational poverty. It lies at the heart of the historical institution of slavery, leaving an indelible mark on the psyche of enslaved people. The legacy of this exploitation continues to reverberate through generations, shaping what is often referred to as a "slave mentality." To comprehend the enduring impact of economic exploitation, it is imperative to examine the historical roots, the psychological toll on them, and their contemporary manifestations.

Slavery, at its core, was an economic system that thrived on the dehumanization of those reduced to mere property. The forced labor of enslaved individuals became the linchpin of this economic machinery, emphasizing profit over the recognition of their humanity. This insidious exploitation formed the economic backbone of the institution, as the fruits of their labor were systematically denied to them. Enslaved individuals, regarded as commodities rather than people, endured not only the theft of their labor but also the infliction of inhumane working conditions. Their toil was extracted in fields, mines, or within households, all with the overarching goal of enriching the slaveholders.

Economic exploitation during slavery had profound psychological consequences for the enslaved population. The denial of economic agency and the fruits of their labor contributed to a sense of powerlessness and diminished self-worth. The enslaved were systematically dehumanized, and treated as commodities rather than with inherent value. The psychological toll extended beyond the immediate experience of exploitation. The intergenerational transmission of trauma meant that the effects of economic exploitation lingered, influencing the mindset of descendants. The legacy of being treated as property rather than free and autonomous contributed to the development of a slave mentality characterized by feelings of inferiority, learned helplessness, and a belief in the inherent inequality of certain groups. The economic benefits reaped from the enslaved population's labor served to consolidate power and wealth within the hands of the slaveholders, creating a socio-economic landscape where disparities were not only tolerated but institutionalized. This entrenchment of economic inequality became deeply woven into the social fabric, setting the stage for the persistence of economic disparities and the perpetuation of a slave mentality long after the formal abolition of slavery.

While formal slavery has been abolished, the echoes of economic exploitation persist in contemporary society. The vestiges of historical injustices are evident in systemic inequalities that disproportionately affect certain communities. Economic disparities, often along racial lines, continue to perpetuate cycles of poverty and limited access to opportunities. The contemporary manifestations of economic exploitation contribute to the persistence of a slave mentality among marginalized communities. Limited access to quality education, employment discrimination, and unequal economic opportunities create barriers that reinforce the narrative of inherent inferiority. The psychological impact of historical economic exploitation continues to shape the collective consciousness, influencing attitudes toward self-worth, success, and the possibility of upward mobility.

Breaking free from the shackles of economic exploitation and the associated slave mentality requires a multifaceted approach. Education emerges as a powerful tool, providing people with the knowledge and skills necessary to challenge systemic inequalities. Moreover, economic empowerment, through initiatives such as entrepreneurship and community development, can counteract the effects of historical exploitation by fostering economic self-sufficiency and resilience. Policy interventions are crucial in dismantling systemic barriers that perpetuate economic exploitation. Affirmative action, anti-discrimination laws, and targeted economic initiatives can help address historical inequities and create a more level playing field. Recognizing the intersectionality of economic exploitation with other forms of oppression, such as racism and sexism, is essential for developing comprehensive and effective solutions.

Social Conflict:

Social conflict is a multifaceted phenomenon that encapsulates the dynamic tension, disagreement, or discord prevalent in societies when individuals or groups find themselves at odds due to opposing interests, values, or goals. This inherent clash of perspectives and objectives can manifest in a spectrum of ways, ranging from peaceful protests, intellectual debates, and advocacy to more intense and even violent expressions, such as clashes, demonstrations, and civil unrest. At its core, social conflict serves as a barometer for the divergent forces at play within a society, reflecting the intricate interplay of competing interests and values.

Disparities in wealth, power, and access to resources are prominent catalysts for social conflict. When certain segments of a population perceive or experience inequality in economic opportunities, social mobility, or resource distribution, it often results in heightened tensions and discontent. The perceived or actual unequal distribution of these crucial elements can trigger social movements, protests, or even upheavals as individuals or groups strive to rectify perceived injustices and reshape the societal landscape.

Social conflict can emanate from cultural, religious, or ideological disputes, as differences in beliefs and values often become flashpoints for discord. These disagreements may lead to social fragmentation, with communities or groups asserting their identity and challenging competing narratives. Cultural clashes, religious tensions, and ideological differences can fuel social conflict, fostering a climate where divergent perspectives vie for prominence and influence. Another potent catalyst for social conflict can be the perception of injustice. When individuals or groups believe that they are being treated unfairly or are denied basic rights and opportunities, a sense of discontent arises, sparking collective action in the form of social movements or protests. This pursuit of justice becomes a driving force behind social conflict, compelling them to challenge established norms, demand change, and push for the realization of more equality and inclusive societal structures.

Conflict, as an inherent facet of human interaction, carries the potential for both constructive and destructive outcomes, shaping the trajectory of societies in profound ways. Constructive conflict serves as a catalyst for positive change, acting as a driving force behind social evolution, dialogue, and the dismantling of inadequate systems. In this form, conflict becomes a crucible for innovation and growth, challenging established norms and sparking discussions that can lead to meaningful transformations within a society. The clash of ideas and perspectives inherent in constructive conflict creates an environment where diverse voices are heard, fostering a pluralistic society that embraces change and adaptation. Alternatively, when conflict is left unresolved or escalates beyond constructive boundaries, its consequences can be detrimental, leading to division, violence, and social upheaval. Unchecked conflict can fracture the social fabric, deepening existing fissures and creating new fault lines within communities. The repercussions of such escalation often extend far beyond the immediate moment, leaving a lasting impact on the cohesion and stability of a society. Social divisions, once exacerbated by uncontrolled conflict, may persist, hindering collaboration and impeding the pursuit of shared goals.

Violent manifestations of conflict, whether interpersonal or societal, can inflict severe trauma, leaving scars that endure across generations. The aftermath of unbridled conflict may include the erosion of trust, the breakdown of social institutions, and a sense of collective disillusionment. Societies grappling with the aftermath of intense conflict often face the arduous task of rebuilding not only physical infrastructure but also the social and psychological bonds that have been strained or shattered. However, recognizing the dual nature of conflict underscores the importance of proactive and constructive approaches to conflict resolution. Embracing dialogue, mediation, and negotiation as tools for addressing conflicts can help mitigate the negative consequences associated with escalating discord. Constructive conflict resolution fosters a culture of compromise, understanding, and reconciliation, enabling societies to navigate differences without resorting to destructive means.

Intersectionality:

Intersectionality is a concept first introduced by Kimberlé Crenshaw which provides a lens through which to understand the intricate and multifaceted experiences of people, particularly within the historical context of slavery. In examining intersectionality in relation to slavery, it becomes evident that the oppression faced was not a monolithic experience; rather, it was shaped by the intersection of various identities, including race, gender, class, and more. This notion attempts to shed light on the nuanced dynamics that characterized the lives of those subjected to the brutal institution of slavery.

The institution of slavery was a complex system that exploited based on race, heritage, class, ethnicity, and other factors, but the experiences of enslaved people were further complicated by the intersections of their identities. For instance, enslaved women faced a unique set of challenges, as their oppression was not only rooted in racial discrimination but also intertwined with gender-based exploitation. The intersection of race and gender created a compounded form of oppression, leading to distinct challenges that necessitate a nuanced understanding. Enslaved women, while enduring the dehumanization and brutality experienced by all slaves, also faced the additional burden of sexual exploitation. They were subjected to both physical and sexual violence, highlighting how the intersection of race and gender magnified their vulnerability. This intersectional lens allows us to appreciate the specific struggles faced by enslaved women, illustrating that the institution of slavery was not a uniform experience for all people.

Class was another dimension that intersected with race within the context of slavery. Enslaved individuals were not a homogenous group; rather, they occupied various economic positions within the slave-owning society. The intersections of race and class created a hierarchy among the enslaved, with those in more privileged positions often acting as overseers or skilled laborers, while others toiled in harsh conditions on plantations. The economic disparities among them further complicated their experiences. Those in more privileged positions might have been shielded from some of the more extreme forms of physical brutality, but they still grappled with the psychological toll of being enslaved. Recognizing these nuances through an intersectional lens allows us to understand how economic disparities within the enslaved population were shaped by the intersecting forces of race and class.

The intersectionality of slavery also had profound effects on family structures. The separation of families through the sale of the enslaved was a common practice, and the emotional toll on families was devastating. The intersection of race and familial relationships deepened the psychological scars, as enslaved people not only faced personal dehumanization but also witnessed the fragmentation of their families. Furthermore, the experience of parenthood within the context of slavery was fraught with challenges. Enslaved mothers, in particular, faced the heart-wrenching reality of knowing that their children could be taken away at any moment. This intersection of race, gender, and family roles highlights the complex emotional landscape in which they navigated their lives.

Intersectionality is a comprehensive and nuanced framework that elucidates the intricate ways in which people experience and navigate systems of oppression and discrimination. At its core, intersectionality posits that people are not subject to a singular form of discrimination but rather encounter intersecting and overlapping layers of oppression based on various facets of their identity. These dimensions encompass but are not limited to race, gender, class, sexuality, disability, and other social categories, creating a complex web of experiences that cannot be fully understood or addressed by examining each aspect in isolation, they are viewed as embodying multiple and interconnected identities, each of which contributes to their overall social positioning. The experiences of discrimination and disadvantage are not additive but synergistic, as the intersection of different identities can result in unique and compounded forms of marginalization. For example, a woman of color may face challenges that are distinct from those encountered by a white woman or a man of color, highlighting the need to consider the intersection of race and gender in understanding her experiences. A black woman may experience discrimination differently from a white woman or a black man, as she faces the unique challenges of being both a woman and a person of color. It emphasizes the importance of considering the complex and overlapping dimensions of identity when analyzing issues of social justice and equality. It emphasizes that people's experiences and vulnerabilities cannot be understood by examining a single aspect of their identity in isolation. This framework has become central to discussions on addressing systemic inequalities and advocating for more inclusive and uniformed policies and practices. Intersectionality also underscores the inadequacy of single-issue approaches to social justice, as these approaches may overlook the complex ways in which different forms of discrimination intersect and reinforce each other. In theory, by adopting an intersectional lens, activists, scholars, and policymakers can develop more comprehensive and inclusive strategies for addressing systemic inequalities, ensuring that efforts are attuned to the multifaceted nature of individuals' identities and experiences.

Intersectionality in the context of slavery unveils the intricate layers of oppression faced by people whose lives were profoundly shaped by this institution. Recognizing the intersections of race, gender, class, and family roles provides a more nuanced understanding of the varied experiences within the enslaved population. This nuanced perspective is believed to be crucial for historical accuracy and also informs contemporary efforts to address the lasting impact of slavery on marginalized communities. An intersectional approach allows us to navigate the complexities of the past and present, fostering a future with equality of opportunities. Conveniently, it does not take into consideration that every community has to deal with the adversities of slavery at some point. However, it is crucial in understanding the mindsets that are the foundation of philosophy.

Final Thoughts

The philosophy of subordination is a multifaceted and contentious concept that permeates various aspects of society, from politics and economics to culture and identity. While some argue that certain forms of subordination are necessary for maintaining order, others view it as a profound injustice that must be addressed and eradicated. As societies evolve, discussions around subordination continue to be central to efforts aimed at achieving equality, justice, and human rights for all. Acknowledging the complexities and controversies surrounding this philosophy is essential for fostering a world with equality

Recognizing the potential constructive applications of the philosophy of subordination in promoting personal responsibility and empowerment, it is essential to acknowledge its capacity to also exacerbate a victim mentality. This inclination can lead to numerous adverse consequences for both individuals and societies. Among these detrimental effects are dependency, a diminished sense of agency, and resentment towards others or entire communities. The philosophy erodes self-esteem and fosters stagnation, impacting both individual growth and community development. Individuals adopting a victim mentality may become entrenched in their beliefs, actively seeking confirmation of their victim status while dismissing information that challenges this perspective. Such a mindset can perpetuate a distorted worldview, discouraging engagement in advocacy or social change initiatives due to feelings of disempowerment and hopelessness. Additionally, it hinders effective problem-solving by prioritizing assigning blame over seeking solutions, thus perpetuating the very problems it aims to address.

The concept of Intersectionality, in particular, is very interesting, especially as it pertains to slavery and the slave mentality. While intersectionality is still making its way into acceptance through education, it is important to scrutinize its application in the context of slavery. While acknowledging the different dimensions of identity may be valuable, I would argue that the application of intersectionality to the historical experiences of slavery oversimplifies the intricate dynamics at play during this dark period of human history. Applying contemporary frameworks such as intersectionality to historical contexts may impose modern perspectives on societies vastly different from our own. Slavery, as an institution, operated within a distinct social and economic structure that defies easy categorization through contemporary lenses. Attempting to superimpose intersectional analysis onto the historical realities of slavery risks oversimplifying the complex power dynamics and social hierarchies that existed. Additionally, the intersectional lens may inadvertently overshadow the common humanity of those who suffered under slavery. By focusing on the intersections of identity, there is a risk of neglecting the shared experiences of dehumanization, loss of agency, and brutality that affected every slave throughout all of the denominations, not just the ones necessary to advance agendas. Emphasizing on differences within the enslaved population may obscure the fundamental injustice that was universally experienced. The use of intersectionality can also lead to a fragmented understanding of historical events. By isolating and analyzing specific aspects of identity, there is a risk of losing sight of the interconnected nature of historical realities. For example, emphasizing the intersection of race and gender may overlook the economic disparities or familial disruptions that were integral components of the slave experience. Critics argue that a more holistic approach is necessary to grasp the full complexity of the historical narrative.

While intersectionality has yet to prove its value in contemporary analyses of social structures, therefore its application to the historical context of slavery must also not be met with disputation. There is a certain risk of anachronism and oversimplification. Perhaps a better option is a degree of nuanced and contextually sensitive approaches that preserve the multifaceted nature of the institution of slavery without reducing it to isolated intersections of identity.

Chapter Four: The Correlation Between Victim Mentality and Slave Mentality

Victim Mentality vs Slave Mentality

The correlation between victim mentality and slave mentality is a complex and nuanced concept that warrants examination. While these two mindsets share some similarities, they also differ in certain ways. We have established that the victim mentality is a psychological phenomenon where they perceive themselves as victims of external circumstances or forces. This mindset often involves a tendency to attribute one's problems to external factors, such as other people, societal systems, or fate, rather than taking personal responsibility for one's actions or choices. People with a victim mentality may focus on past grievances and difficulties, often seeking sympathy and validation from others. This mindset can lead to feelings of helplessness and chronic negativity.

Victim mentality can be demonstrated in various personal and societal contexts. In milder forms, people may use this mindset as a means to deal with the difficulties they face, seeking validation or sympathy from others. However, when victim mentality becomes pervasive and self-limiting, it can hinder personal growth, resilience, and well-being. Slave mentality, on the other hand, emerged within the harrowing context of historical slavery a system marked by the cruel dehumanization and brutal oppression. Enslaved people endured extreme physical and psychological abuse, were denied legal rights, and had little personal agency. The term "slave mentality" refers to the mindset that developed as a survival mechanism under these dire conditions. Some of the key characteristics of slave mentality include submission to authority, endurance, and a profound sense of powerlessness. Enslaved individuals had to adapt to their circumstances and find ways to cope with the horrors of slavery. Resistance was often met with severe punishment, making submissions to authority as a pragmatic choice for survival.

Contrary to the prevailing notion that emphasizes the importance of acknowledging inherent differences between the victim mentality and slave mentality, I take a divergent stance, contending that these mindsets are not mutually exclusive but rather interchangeable, capable of coexisting and even working in tandem. Both the victim mentality and slave mentality, despite historical and contextual disparities, exhibit commonalities rooted in a shared sense of perceived powerlessness and subjugation, stemming from analogous sets of conditions. It, often discussed in a contemporary psychological context, characterizes a propensity to attribute challenges exclusively to external forces, avoiding personal responsibility and agency. On the other hand, the slave mentality draws from historical and socio-cultural contexts, symbolizing the mindset of those subjected to oppression, exploitation, and subjugation. While the origins and manifestations of these mentalities may differ, a critical examination reveals an intersection of themes related to powerlessness and a perceived lack of control over one's circumstances. The interchangeable nature of these mentalities becomes apparent when considering the psychological impact of external conditions that contribute to feelings of helplessness. Both mindsets arise from environments characterized by systemic inequalities, limited opportunities, and structures that perpetuate subjugation. Whether it be the historical enslavement of a population or the modern dynamics that foster a victim mentality, the shared thread lies in the disempowerment experienced by individuals caught in these circumstances.

Acknowledging the interchangeability of these mentalities does not diminish the historical and contextual specificities of the victim and slave mentalities. Instead, it invites a nuanced understanding that, despite distinct origins, they can coexist and even reinforce each other under certain conditions. This perspective encourages a comprehensive examination of the societal factors that contribute to the perpetuation of these mindsets, emphasizing the importance of addressing systemic issues to break the cycle of disempowerment.

In essence, challenging the conventional wisdom that emphasizes the distinctiveness of the victim and slave mentalities opens the door to a more nuanced understanding of the complex interplay between one's psychology and broader societal structures. It prompts a consideration of how shared elements of powerlessness can transcend historical and cultural boundaries, offering insights into the collective human experience of navigating challenging circumstances.

Historical Context

The argument can be made that the most profound distinction lies in the historical context. Slave mentality developed during a dark period in human history when millions of people were enslaved solely based on their race, and subjected to systemic and institutionalized dehumanization. Enslaved individuals were stripped of their humanity and forced to endure unimaginable suffering, making their powerlessness a tragic reality. Victim mentality, on the other hand, emerges in contemporary contexts where they, although facing challenges and difficulties, often retain legal rights, access to resources, and the ability to advocate for change within democratic societies. The perception of powerlessness in victim mentality is rooted in personal challenges or societal inequalities, rather than the systemic and institutionalized oppression of slavery.

It could also be argued that slave mentality could only exist because of victim mentality. At the same time, victim mentality can derive from slave mentality. The interplay between slave mentality and victim mentality represents a complex and cyclical relationship that has deep historical roots. One could argue that slave mentality and victim mentality are mutually reinforcing, each contributing to the perpetuation of the other. The longevity of slavery across millennia was, in part, sustained by the psychological conditioning of the enslaved individuals, who were made to internalize their subordinate status. To maintain control, those subjected to slavery had to believe in their own subjugation, accepting it as an immutable aspect of their identity. This psychological manipulation created a pervasive slave mentality that justified and normalized the institution of slavery. They had to believe that there were no other solutions for survival. The belief in victimhood can be limiting, affecting one's perception of available opportunities and personal agency. This parallels the historical context where the enslaved were conditioned to believe that their survival and identity were intrinsically linked to their subjugation. Even in contemporary society, those who harbor a victim mentality may not fully utilize their capabilities, even in democratic settings where opportunities for personal and collective empowerment are ostensibly available. This self-imposed limitation is rooted in the belief that the system, despite its democratic ideals, is not designed to benefit them. They are only for the oppressors... or the slave masters.

The Severity of Perceived Oppression

It can be argued that the severity of oppression experienced by the enslaved far surpasses those that are commonly associated with victim mentality. Enslaved people endured forced labor, physical abuse, family separation, and the denial of basic human rights. Their experiences were characterized by systematic and institutionalized dehumanization and cruelty. In contrast, those with a victim mentality, while feeling powerless, generally face fewer extreme challenges and difficulties. Their perceived powerlessness stems from personal struggles or societal issues within a democratic framework, where they still maintain the potential for advocacy, change, and legal redress. Though that may be true, it ignores the power of perception of oppression which can be described as the subjective belief held by individuals or groups that they are experiencing unjust treatment, discrimination, or disadvantage based on various factors such as race, gender, religion, sexuality, or social status when pertaining oppression. This perception is often rooted in their experiences and interpretation of societal interactions, policies, or practices. The reality of a person who perceives personal oppression is no different from the reality of a slave. The difference between the subjective state and the objective state can only be made, unfortunately, by the outside observer. The slave is a slave to a master in a system created for enslavement. The person who perceives oppression sees themselves as slaves to a system.

The experience of perceived oppression encompasses a range of emotional and psychological responses, each contributing to the complex tapestry of an individual's or group's mental landscape. Among the myriad of ways in which this oppression can manifest, feelings of frustration, anger, helplessness, and resentment are particularly prominent. These emotions arise as a natural response to the perceived existence of systemic barriers or biases that they believe impede their opportunities, rights, or overall quality of life. Feelings of frustration often stem from the idea that despite personal efforts and capabilities, systemic structures may hinder progress and advancement. This frustration may be compounded by the belief that achieving certain goals or accessing certain opportunities is unfairly challenging due to societal biases or discriminatory practices. Anger may emerge as a visceral response to the perceived injustice and inequality, reflecting a deep-seated desire for change and redress. Helplessness can pervade the mindset of those who feel oppressed, especially when faced with formidable institutional barriers. The belief that one's efforts may be futile in the face of inequalities can lead to a sense of powerlessness, contributing to a cycle of disenchantment and disengagement. This feeling of helplessness may further exacerbate mental distress and impact overall well-being. Resentment, rooted in the perception of being unjustly treated or marginalized, can be a potent emotion in the context of perceived oppression. The ongoing awareness of systemic biases may fuel a sense of bitterness, eroding trust in societal structures and institutions. This emotional response can have far-reaching consequences, affecting interpersonal relationships and shaping one's outlook on broader societal dynamics. The psychological impact of perceived oppression extends beyond the realm of emotions to deeply affect their self-esteem, mental well-being, and overall life satisfaction. Constant exposure to systemic barriers and biases can erode one's confidence and self-worth, leading to a negative self-perception. Mental health may be compromised as they grapple with the stressors associated with navigating an unjust system, potentially leading to conditions such as anxiety or depression. Are we to believe slaves didn't harbor the same sentiments?

The severity of perceived oppression is rooted in the psychological toll it takes on individuals. The constant awareness of being oppressed, discriminated against, or marginalized can lead to chronic stress, anxiety, and a diminished sense of self-worth. Psychologically, the weight of perceived oppression manifests in various ways, including heightened vigilance, hypervigilance, and the internalization of negative societal narratives. The experience of perceived oppression often triggers a fight-or-flight response, even in situations where physical danger may not be imminent. This chronic state of alertness can contribute to mental fatigue, emotional exhaustion, and a sense of powerlessness. The emotional toll of perceived oppression can be particularly profound, leading to feelings of anger, frustration, and despair. Internalization of negative societal narratives is another psychological dimension of perceived oppression. Those who perceive themselves as oppressed may internalize stereotypes, biases, and negative perceptions projected onto their social group. This internalization can contribute to the development of a negative self-concept, perpetuating a cycle of self-doubt and reinforcing the severity of perceived oppression.

The severity of perceived oppression has ripple effects on interpersonal relationships and societal dynamics. At the interpersonal level, the emotional toll of perceived oppression can strain relationships, as people navigate the challenges of carrying the weight of their experiences. Trust issues, difficulty forming connections, and a sense of isolation may result from the psychological impact of perceived oppression. Within society, the severity of perceived oppression contributes to broader social dynamics, influencing the discourse around justice, equity, and inclusion. Movements for social change often emerge from the collective experiences of perceived oppression, as marginalized groups unite to demand recognition, rights, and systemic change. However, the severity of perceived oppression can also contribute to polarization and social divisions. When individuals and groups feel deeply oppressed, there is a risk of creating an "us versus them" narrative, hindering constructive dialogue and collaboration. This polarization can impede progress toward a more just and inclusive society, perpetuating a cycle of perceived oppression and resistance. On the other hand, perceived oppression can also lead to narratives marked by internalized stigma, where they may internalize negative societal perceptions and view themselves through the lens of those biases. This internalization can create a self-fulfilling prophecy, influencing behavior, choices, and life outcomes.

The concept of intersectionality adds a layer of complexity to the severity of perceived oppression. Since it claims, or alleges, that people may experience multiple forms of oppression simultaneously based on various intersecting factors, such as race, gender, sexuality, and socio-economic status. This intersectional perspective highlights the unique challenges faced by those who navigate the intersections of different axes of oppression. For example, a person who experiences both racial and gender-based oppression may carry a heavier burden of perceived oppression due to the compounded effects of intersecting identities. Understanding and addressing the complexity of intersectionality is crucial for developing nuanced approaches to social justice and acknowledging the severity of perceived oppression within diverse communities. Once again, this concept ignores the option of the oppression itself being subjective and not objective in nature.

Breaking the cycle of perceived oppression requires a multifaceted approach that addresses both individual and systemic factors. Psychologically, fostering resilience is essential to mitigate the impact of perceived oppression on mental health. This involves providing people with tools to cope with stress, building supportive communities, and promoting mental health awareness. Empowerment through education is a powerful tool for breaking the cycle of perceived oppression. Education can provide them with the knowledge and skills to challenge systemic injustices, question biased narratives, and advocate for change. By fostering critical thinking and empowering them to question oppressive structures, education becomes a catalyst for breaking the cycle of perceived oppression. At the societal level, dismantling systemic barriers and promoting equality are crucial steps in addressing the severity of perceived oppression. Policies that ensure equal opportunities, challenge discriminatory practices, and foster inclusivity based on the merits of one's deeds will greatly contribute to creating a more just and equal society. Moreover, fostering empathy and understanding among diverse communities is essential for breaking down societal divisions fueled by perceived oppression. Building bridges of communication, actively listening to different perspectives, and acknowledging the diverse experiences of oppression contribute to creating a more cohesive and supportive society. Moreover, fostering empathy and understanding among diverse communities is essential for breaking down societal divisions fueled by perceived oppression. Building bridges of communication, actively listening to different perspectives, and acknowledging the diverse experiences of oppression contribute to creating a more cohesive and supportive society.

The severity of perceived oppression is a complex and multifaceted phenomenon that extends beyond individual experiences to shape interpersonal relationships and societal dynamics. Understanding the psychological dimensions, its impact on personal narratives, and the intersectionality of perceived oppression is essential for developing comprehensive strategies to address its profound effects. Breaking the cycle of perceived oppression requires a concerted effort at the individual and societal levels. Fostering resilience, empowering through education, and dismantling systemic barriers are crucial steps in creating a more just and equal society. By acknowledging the severity of perceived oppression and working collaboratively toward positive change, society can move toward a future marked by empathy, inclusivity, and justice.

Coping Mechanisms:

We can agree that both mindsets involve coping mechanisms, and they do not differ in nature and purpose. Some may say that those with a victim mentality may adopt coping mechanisms like self-pity, external attribution, or seeking sympathy to navigate their challenges or grievances. These mechanisms, while not always constructive, provide a sense of relief or validation while the enslaved developed coping mechanisms out of necessity to survive the horrors of slavery. Their coping strategies, such as submission to authority, endurance, and the formation of supportive communities within the enslaved population, were rooted in minimizing harm and maintaining a semblance of agency within the oppressive system.

Learned helplessness, was coined by psychologists Martin Seligman and Steven Maier in the 1960s, based on their research with animals, and it has since been applied to the study of human behavior. This phenomenon has profound implications for understanding human behavior, motivation, mental health, and even social issues like poverty, depression, and the perpetuation of perceived oppression. It is a pervasive negative coping mechanism that is closely linked to the slave mentality. It occurs when they feel powerless and believe they have no control over their lives or circumstances. This feeling of powerlessness can stem from generations of oppression and systemic discrimination, where escape from such conditions was nearly impossible. One of the most detrimental effects of learned helplessness is that it fosters a sense of apathy. When people believe they cannot change their situation, they may become complacent and unwilling to take the initiative to improve their lives. This coping mechanism can perpetuate cycles of poverty, underachievement, and a lack of self-empowerment within marginalized communities. At its core, learned helplessness is a belief system that develops when people perceive their actions as ineffective in controlling or influencing the outcomes in their lives. It arises from a history of experiencing negative events or outcomes, particularly those that seem beyond one's control. For example, a person who is repeatedly subjected to adversity, discrimination, or systemic oppression may eventually develop a belief that their efforts to change their situation are futile. The classic experiment that demonstrated learned helplessness in animals involved subjecting dogs to inescapable electric shocks. Over time, the dogs stopped trying to escape, even when an opportunity to do so was presented, because they had "learned" that their actions did not affect the outcome. This study laid the foundation for understanding how humans, too, can develop a sense of helplessness when they perceive that their actions have no impact on the situations they face.

Learned helplessness is a complex and profound psychological concept that has far-reaching implications for individuals and societies. Understanding how it develops and affects various aspects of life is a critical step toward breaking the cycle and regaining a sense of control and agency. Breaking free from learned helplessness requires self-awareness, cognitive restructuring, goal setting, support, and resilience building. In the context of systemic issues, it may also involve advocacy and activism to challenge and change the structures that perpetuate cycles of oppression and inequality. By recognizing learned helplessness and taking steps to overcome it, they can reclaim their power and work toward a more empowered, fulfilling, and purposeful life.

Slave mentality often leads to a sense of perpetual victimhood. This negative coping mechanism involves constantly viewing oneself as a victim of external forces including racism, discrimination, and other injustices. It is the psychological state of perceiving oneself as a perpetual victim, where adversity and setbacks are attributed to external forces, rather than being recognized as challenges to overcome.

While acknowledging these issues is crucial, adopting a perpetual victim mentality can lead to a cycle of self-pity, resentment, and a lack of personal responsibility. Perpetual victimhood can prevent people from taking agency over their own lives and making necessary changes. It may lead to a belief that success is unattainable because the world is fundamentally against them. This mindset can be deeply ingrained and has far-reaching consequences, influencing not only their sense of self-worth and personal development but also affecting interpersonal relationships, mental health, and societal dynamics. Breaking free from this negative coping mechanism requires a shift towards empowerment and a recognition of one's own ability to overcome adversity.

Perpetual victimhood, which can often be referred to as a victim mentality, is a psychological state where people consistently see themselves as victims of external circumstances, other people, or the world at large. It is a mindset rooted in the belief that one's life is largely shaped by external factors, such as unfair treatment, discrimination, or systemic oppression, rather than their agency or choices. This mindset often stems from a history of real or perceived victimization. Those who have faced significant challenges or adversity may develop a victim mentality as a coping mechanism. By attributing their difficulties to external causes, they can avoid taking responsibility for their own actions or circumstances.

Perpetual victimhood can manifest in various ways, and its effects may be subtle or overt. Blame Shifting, helplessness, negative self-concept and avoidance of responsibilities are just a few manifestations. While this mindset often arises as a coping mechanism in response to adversity and trauma, it can hinder personal growth, mental health, and relationships. Breaking free from perpetual victimhood requires self-awareness, self-reflection, and a commitment to taking responsibility for one's choices and circumstances. Overcoming this mindset is a journey towards personal empowerment and resilience, allowing them to face life's challenges with a sense of agency and optimism. On a societal level, recognizing the role that perpetuating victimhood plays in social dynamics can lead to more constructive approaches to addressing systemic issues and fostering unity and self-empowerment. Ultimately, breaking free from a victim mentality is a transformative process that can lead to personal growth and well-being.

The scarcity mindset is a psychological phenomenon characterized by a pervasive belief that resources, opportunities, and even time are inherently limited. Those who adopt this mindset often perceive the world as a zero-sum game, where one person's gain necessarily equates to another's loss. It can manifest in various aspects of life, from financial decisions to interpersonal relationships, and it can have significant consequences for a person's well-being and personal growth. This mindset is often rooted in experiences of lack, poverty, or limited access to resources during childhood or adulthood. It can also be influenced by societal and cultural factors, as well as external pressures. When they constantly perceive scarcity in their lives, they may develop a deep-seated fear of not having enough. As a result, they may exhibit various behaviors and thought patterns that reflect this mindset.

One of the key manifestations of a scarcity mindset is a continuous focus on what one lacks rather than what one has. This can lead to a preoccupation with material possessions, leading to hoarding, excessive saving, and fear of spending, even when it's necessary. Such behaviors can hinder personal financial growth, as people may avoid investing in opportunities or experiences that could potentially lead to improvement. In relationships, this mindset can lead to possessiveness, jealousy, and a reluctance to share emotional or material resources. This can strain connections with friends and loved ones, as they may view the world as a competitive place where sharing could result in personal loss. Over time, this perspective can erode trust and damage the quality of relationships. Furthermore, it can inhibit personal and professional growth. The belief that opportunities are scarce can lead to hesitation and reluctance to take risks or seek new experiences. This fear of scarcity can hold them back from pursuing their goals, as they may avoid stepping outside their comfort zones or seeking education and personal development.

Overcoming a scarcity mindset is a transformative process that requires a shift in one's perspective. It begins with self-awareness and recognizing the limiting beliefs and behaviors that stem from this mindset. Understanding that the world is not a zero-sum game and that resources can be abundant with the right approach is crucial. Changing this mindset involves developing financial literacy and discipline. People can learn to differentiate between necessary and excessive spending, prioritize savings and investments, and gradually build financial security. Seeking financial education or professional advice can be beneficial in this regard. In relationships, they can work on fostering trust and cooperation rather than competition. Open communication, sharing, and collaborative decision-making can help build healthier, more meaningful connections with others. When it comes to personal and professional growth, overcoming a scarcity mindset requires taking calculated risks and embracing opportunities for learning and development. This may involve seeking higher education, mentorship, or career advancement. It also involves letting go of the fear that taking these steps will result in personal loss.

Conformity and groupthink are intricate psychological phenomena that profoundly influence human behavior, often without individuals even realizing it. These concepts explore how the need to fit in, maintain group cohesion, and avoid conflict can lead people to abandon their own beliefs, judgment, or values in favor of aligning with a group's consensus. This book delves into conformity and groupthink, shedding light on how they operate, their implications for independent and collective behavior, and strategies to mitigate their influence. Conformity refers to the tendency of people to adjust their thoughts, behaviors, or attitudes to match those of a majority or influential group. It arises from the innate human desire to belong and avoid social rejection. Conformity can manifest in various forms, such as altering one's opinions to align with popular viewpoints, adopting behaviors characteristic of a group, or even going along with decisions against one's better judgment. Psychologists have conducted numerous experiments to understand the dynamics of conformity, perhaps most notably Solomon Asch's experiments on group pressure. Groupthink, on the other hand, is a phenomenon that occurs when a group prioritizes consensus and cohesion over critical thinking and objective evaluation. It often leads to hasty, irrational, or poor decision-making. Groupthink can manifest in diverse contexts, such as corporate boardrooms, political meetings, or even small social gatherings. The term was coined by Irving Janis in the context of analyzing flawed decisions made by groups.

Conformity and groupthink are interrelated, as conformity plays a significant role in the development of groupthink. When people within a group conform to the prevailing opinions or attitudes, it creates a cohesive environment where dissenting views are discouraged. This cohesion, while fostering a sense of belonging, can hinder the group's ability to critically evaluate information and reach well-informed decisions. The implications of conformity and groupthink extend to various aspects of life. In decision-making processes, they can lead to suboptimal choices, missed opportunities, and a failure to consider diverse perspectives. They can also stifle creativity and innovation, as they may suppress their unique ideas in favor of what they perceive to be the group's preference. In political and societal contexts, conformity and groupthink can lead to the perpetuation of harmful ideologies and discrimination. When people conform to prevailing social norms, they may endorse prejudiced views, discriminatory policies, or unjust practices without questioning their ethical implications.

Recognizing the presence of conformity and groupthink in decision-making is the first step toward mitigating their influence. Encouraging open dialogue and diverse perspectives within groups is crucial. It's essential to create an environment where dissent is not only tolerated but actively encouraged, as opposing viewpoints can lead to more thoughtful and informed decisions. Educational institutions can teach critical thinking and problem-solving skills, empowering them to evaluate information objectively and make informed choices. Furthermore, media literacy programs can help them navigate a world where conformity and groupthink can be perpetuated through biased or sensationalized reporting. Societies and communities encouraging inclusivity and diversity of thought are essential in mitigating the harmful consequences of conformity and groupthink. Embracing and celebrating differences can challenge ingrained norms and allow for the exploration of alternative perspectives.

Internalized racism is perhaps one of the most insidious negative coping mechanisms associated with the slave mentality. It is a complex and deeply ingrained phenomenon that occurs when people from racially marginalized communities internalize the negative stereotypes, biases, and discriminatory attitudes directed toward their own racial or ethnic group. This form of self-prejudice can manifest in various ways, impacting self-esteem, self-identity, and interpersonal relationships. Understanding internalized racism is crucial for recognizing and addressing the lasting impact of systemic racism, and it is a significant step toward building a more inclusive and equal society. The roots can be traced back to oppression and discrimination. It occurs when individuals from marginalized racial or ethnic backgrounds are repeatedly exposed to messages that reinforce negative stereotypes and inferiority. Over time, these messages can lead to a sense of self-loathing and a belief in the inherent inferiority of their own racial or ethnic group.

One of the most significant consequences of internalized racism is the development of a negative self-concept. Those who have internalized racist beliefs may struggle with low self-esteem, self-doubt, and feelings of unworthiness. They may question their abilities, potential, and place in society due to the deeply ingrained belief that their racial or ethnic background makes them inferior. It can also manifest in self-deprecation. They may engage in self-criticism, downplay their own achievements, or attribute their successes to external factors rather than recognizing their own abilities and efforts. This self-deprecation can be a significant barrier to personal growth and success. Interpersonal relationships are not immune to the impact of internalized racism. Those who have internalized racist beliefs may view their own racial or ethnic group negatively, leading to strained relationships within their community. They may distance themselves from their cultural heritage or even express disdain for aspects of their own culture or identity. The effects of internalized racism can be particularly pernicious in the realm of identity and self-acceptance. Many people may grapple with questions of belonging and authenticity, feeling like they must conform to dominant cultural norms to be accepted. This can lead to a sense of internal conflict and disconnection from one's own cultural heritage.

Overcoming internalized racism is a complex and ongoing process that often requires individual and collective efforts. Recognizing that these negative self-beliefs are not reflective of one's true worth is a crucial first step. Acknowledging that they have been imposed externally as a result of systemic racism is essential in confronting internalized racism. Building self-esteem and self-worth is an integral part of addressing internalized racism. It involves challenging self-deprecating thoughts, celebrating one's achievements, and recognizing one's intrinsic value as a human being, irrespective of race or ethnicity. Engaging in self-reflection and cultural reconnection can help people find pride in their heritage and cultural identity. This may involve learning about the history and achievements of their racial or ethnic group and actively participating in cultural practices and traditions. Support and community are indispensable resources for overcoming internalized racism. Engaging with supportive communities that share similar experiences can provide a sense of belonging and empowerment. These communities can offer a safe space for dialogue, healing, and growth. Mental health professionals, including therapists and counselors, can provide guidance and support to those who are grappling with internalized racism. These experts can help individuals unpack the deep-seated beliefs and emotions related to their experiences of discrimination.

Escapism is a pervasive human tendency, deeply rooted in the desire to seek solace and relief from the pressures and challenges of everyday life. It manifests in various forms, often involving the pursuit of distraction, entertainment, or fantasy as a means to temporarily evade reality's demands. While escapism can offer a necessary respite and even therapeutic benefits, it also carries the risk of becoming a problematic coping mechanism when used in excess. This essay explores the concept of escapism, its manifestations, its significance, and the potential consequences it may entail. It finds its roots in the human need to alleviate stress and mental fatigue. Life's complexities, responsibilities, and uncertainties can become overwhelming, prompting people to seek refuge in various forms of diversion. These diversions can range from engaging in entertainment like reading, watching films, or playing video games to more immersive experiences, such as daydreaming, indulging in fantasies, or even substance abuse. The common thread is the desire to detach temporarily from reality's constraints and challenges.

One of the most prevalent forms of escapism is through entertainment media. Books, movies, television series, and video games offer individuals the opportunity to step into different worlds, escape into compelling narratives, and identify with fictional characters. This form of escapism provides a much-needed mental break, allowing them to immerse themselves in alternate realities for a brief respite from their everyday concerns. Daydreaming is another common form of escapism. People often engage in elaborate daydreams or fantasies as a means to temporarily transcend the boundaries of their current circumstances. These imaginative scenarios can provide comfort, hope, or an emotional escape, enabling people to cope with stress or uncertainty. For some, substance abuse is a very unfortunate manifestation of escapism. Alcohol, drugs, or other substances, some of which are addictive, are used as a way to numb the mind and temporarily escape from reality. This may provide short-term relief, but it often leads to more significant problems and health consequences, like addiction. It is significant for its ability to offer them a mental break and emotional relief. It can serve as a coping mechanism, helping people regain perspective, reduce stress, and recharge. Engaging in hobbies or activities that provide a temporary escape from everyday concerns can be therapeutic, allowing them to return to their responsibilities with a renewed sense of clarity and resilience. However, the extent to which it is pursued can vary significantly. Excessive escapism, especially when used as a primary coping strategy, can lead to extremely negative consequences. Some may find it challenging to address real-life problems, meet their responsibilities, or engage in meaningful relationships if they become too engrossed in escapism. It can hinder personal growth, potentially leading to a cycle of avoidance rather than proactive problem-solving. Moreover, it can mask underlying emotional or psychological issues. Instead of confronting difficult emotions or challenges head-on, they may use escapism as a means to avoid these issues, ultimately delaying the necessary resolution and potentially exacerbating their impact.

To strike a balance between the benefits and potential drawbacks of escapism, people should practice mindfulness and self-awareness. Recognizing when and why they turn to escapism is a crucial step. It is essential to use escapism as a tool for rejuvenation and relief, rather than as a means of permanent avoidance. Engaging in healthy escapism means setting boundaries, managing time effectively, and addressing responsibilities in a timely manner. It also involves seeking help when needed, especially when escapism becomes a means of avoiding unresolved emotional or psychological issues.

The negative coping mechanisms intertwined with the slave mentality are not isolated occurrences but rather deeply rooted behaviors that have stood the test of time, often transmitted from one generation to the next. These mechanisms have evolved as responses to centuries of systemic oppression, racism, and marginalization. They have not only affected lives but have also shaped entire communities and societies. Recognizing and addressing these mechanisms is not only an urgent call for personal transformation but also an indispensable step toward collective healing and societal progress. The consequences of these coping mechanisms extend far beyond personal experiences, influencing the dynamics of communities, institutions, and nations. In the broader context, these mechanisms manifest as institutional racism, and disparities in education, employment, and criminal justice, perpetuating cycles of inequality that affect marginalized groups for generations.

A commitment to breaking free from the limitations imposed by the past is not a simple task but a lifelong journey. It requires resilience, determination, and a willingness to endure discomfort as old beliefs and behaviors are challenged. Breaking free from these mechanisms is not just a personal journey but a societal imperative. It means working to dismantle the systemic structures that have perpetuated these mechanisms for generations. By doing so, individuals can unlock their full potential, leading to personal growth, self-empowerment, and the ability to contribute positively to their communities. It is through this transformation that individuals can begin to challenge the structural inequalities that persist in society. Only by collectively recognizing, addressing, and dismantling these negative coping mechanisms can we hope to build a more just and equal world, where the vestiges of the slave mentality no longer hold sway over the lives of marginalized individuals and communities. In this process of change, we forge a path toward a more inclusive, empathetic, and compassionate society, one that values the dignity and potential of everyone.

Final Thoughts

The true slave has fully submitted to the person, persons, or system that enslaves them and, in fact, will fight and defend the furtherance of their enslavers over the fear of being separated. The slave will always seek their master's, or capture's, approval as a trade-off for the instant gratification of satisfying the master or captor. The irony is that it is our own survival instinct that perpetuates this deathlike mindset. Understanding the complicated interactions of all of the components of both syndromes can only help in the effort to irradicate Slave Mentality altogether. The human psyche, shaped by an innumerable quantity of experiences and influences, sometimes manifests in patterns of thought and behavior that reflect a sense of victimhood or subjugation. Two such psychological phenomena are victim mentality and slave mentality. While distinct in their origins, these mentalities share striking similarities that underscore the intricate ways in which they perceive and respond to challenges. While light has been shined on the commonalities between victim mentality and slave mentality, we now have a better understanding of their psychological underpinnings, impact on personal narratives, and implications for breaking free from cycles of disempowerment. While Victim Mentality and Slave Mentality share elements of perceived powerlessness, the severity of subjugation, the historical context, and the agency that they had within their situations significantly differ. The similarities are rooted in the shared perception of powerlessness and the influence of external factors.

In understanding the similarities between victim mentality and slave mentality, a nuanced exploration emerges, revealing the interconnected psychological patterns that contribute to disempowerment. Both mentalities involve a perception of external forces shaping one's destiny, a learned helplessness that hinders personal agency, and the internalization of narratives that perpetuate disempowerment. Breaking free from these mentalities requires a holistic approach that encompasses self-awareness, resilience-building, reframing narratives, and active engagement with supportive communities. Education, advocacy for social justice, and therapeutic interventions can also play pivotal roles in fostering empowerment. By acknowledging the similarities and addressing the root causes, people can embark on a journey towards breaking free from the weight of victim or slave mentalities, reclaiming personal agency, and contributing to a more just and equal society. The process is complex, but the potential for personal growth and societal transformation is profound.

Chapter Five: Mental Shackles

Mental Slavery

In the complicated tapestry of human existence, the concept of mental slavery unveils a profound narrative of psychological subjugation, where the mind, oftentimes unbeknownst to its bearer, becomes ensnared in the invisible chains of oppressive ideologies that bind the mind is the logical outcome of slave mentality and victim mentality. This phenomenon, deeply rooted in historical legacies of institutionalized oppression, transcends time and manifests in contemporary contexts, shaping the way people perceive themselves, their communities, and their place in the world. From the oppressive regimes of colonialism to the enduring effects of cultural hegemony, the historical underpinnings lay bare the intricate ways in which minds have been molded, beliefs have been shaped, and autonomy has been stifled. The invisible chains

Historically, mental slavery finds its roots in the systemic oppression embedded in structures such as colonialism and slavery. These institutions were not only marked by physical subjugation but also by a calculated erosion of cultural identities. The imposition of foreign norms, values, and belief systems sought to strip people of their intrinsic identities, fostering a sense of inferiority and subordination. Cultural hegemony, a powerful force that reinforces the dominance of a ruling class's cultural narratives, perpetuated mental slavery by shaping their perceptions and limiting their capacity to envision alternatives beyond the established narrative.

Education is intended as a beacon of enlightenment, ironically became a tool of indoctrination. The deliberate shaping of curricula and historical narratives allowed those in power to mold minds, perpetuating mental slavery through biased information and distorted perspectives. The very essence of learning becomes tainted, reinforcing narratives that subjugate certain communities while glorifying oppressive ideology. Critical Race Theory comes to mind. By teaching that children of one target community that they are oppressed by another target community. The first steps to creating an environment that encourages and reinforces perceived oppression and hate have been initiated. The role of media, particularly in the digital age, cannot be overlooked. Mass media perpetuates mental slavery through biased portrayals, stereotyping, and the underrepresentation of diverse voices. The very platforms designed to connect them worldwide can become breeding grounds for cyberbullying, the spread of harmful stereotypes, and the influence of curated online personas. Technological advancements, while offering connectivity, also pose risks to mental autonomy. Mass surveillance and data collection create a pervasive sense of being constantly monitored, fostering self-censorship and inhibiting the free exchange of ideas. Social media, a double-edged sword, provides spaces for expression but can also become arenas for the perpetuation of mental slavery, contributing to the shaping of their self-perception.

It is evident that mental slavery is not confined to the past; it reverberates through contemporary societies as well. Its manifestations are refined, adapting to the ever-evolving dynamics of the modern world. Colorism and beauty standards become conduits for mental subjugation, as people internalize notions of beauty that align with oppressive norms, rejecting their natural features. The Hutu and Totsi are the perfect example of this. The subjugation of one by the other and an oppressive regime led to a civil war and genocide. Language and cultural erasure perpetuate mental slavery by disconnecting them from their cultural roots, contributing to a sense of cultural inferiority. Religious institutions, when co-opted by oppressive regimes, transform into instruments of mental subjugation. The imposition of a specific religious doctrine may reinforce hierarchical power structures, discouraging critical thinking and fostering unquestioning obedience.

Economic exploitation, another contemporary facet of mental slavery, restricts access to resources and opportunities based on socioeconomic status, leading to the internalization of economic inequality and a resignation of the established social order.

Victim Mentality to Perpetuate Mental Shackles

Remember, victim mentality is a psychological state where people perceive themselves as perpetual victims, can become an unwitting accomplice in the perpetuation of mental shackles. The human psyche is a very intricate scene and can described as a nuanced psychological state. When manipulated, it becomes a potent instrument in perpetuating mental shackles amongst other conditions and restrictions. While acknowledging and empathizing with genuine experiences of hardship is essential, the insidious exploitation of victim mentality engenders a self-defeating cycle that reinforces disempowerment. There are multifaceted techniques and methodologies by which victim mentality can be harnessed to perpetuate mental shackles, unraveling the psychological mechanisms, external influences, and the profound impact on personal narratives.

At its core, victim mentality involves perceiving oneself as a perpetual victim, a posture that can arise from genuine adversity or be manipulated to serve certain agendas. The entanglement of victim mentality in a cycle of disempowerment is marked by the embrace of learned helplessness. Those who internalize victimhood often develop a belief that their circumstances are beyond their control, fostering a sense of powerlessness that becomes a self-fulfilling prophecy. In this context, acknowledging external challenges morphs into a relinquishment of personal agency, and the possibility of change is dismissed as an unattainable ideal. A pivotal aspect of perpetuating mental shackles through victim mentality is the externalization of responsibility. While external factors undoubtedly shape the challenges they face, victim mentality, when exploited, manifests as a perpetual shifting of blame onto others or external circumstances. The constant attribution of difficulties to external sources becomes a potent force that inhibits self-examination, a key element of personal growth and breaking free from mental shackles. The exploitation of victim mentality extends its grasp by creating a cycle of dependency. Those who are entrapped in this mindset often come to rely heavily on external support, be it emotional, financial, or otherwise, without actively seeking avenues for self-improvement. This dependency reinforces the narrative of incapacity, making it challenging to break free from mental shackles and attain a sense of self-sufficiency.

Manipulating collective narratives forms another facet of perpetuating mental shackles through victim mentality. External entities, such as political figures, institutions, or media, may leverage the collective victimhood of a group to advance specific agendas. By amplifying the collective sense of disempowerment, these external influencers further entrench a victim mindset within the group psyche, perpetuating mental shackles across entire communities. Beyond the individual, victimhood can become a collective identity, fostering a sense of belonging through shared suffering. However, when this identity eclipses all other facets of an individual's persona, it transforms into a shackle, restricting personal growth and potential. The exploitation of victim mentality is magnified when victimhood evolves into the primary source of identity, preventing them from envisioning themselves outside the confines of perpetual victimhood. Resistance to personal development becomes a tangible manifestation of perpetuating mental shackles through victim mentality. Those who perceive themselves as victims may actively resist opportunities for education, skill development, or self-improvement due to the belief that change is futile. This resistance, born from a conviction in the impossibility of positive change, solidifies mental shackles by impeding personal growth.

Perpetuating mental shackles through victim mentality also finds expression in self-sabotaging behaviors. The belief in inevitable failure, inherent in victim mentality, manifests in behaviors that undermine a person's potential. Avoiding challenges, procrastination, and undermining one's accomplishments become reinforcing mechanisms that hinder progress and maintain a cycle of disempowerment. Cultivating a culture of blame is another subtle yet potent method employed in perpetuating mental shackles through victim mentality. In environments where victimhood is collectively embraced, blame becomes the default response to challenges. This culture of blame reinforces the belief that external forces are solely responsible for their difficulties, inhibiting a proactive approach to problem-solving and maintaining a cycle of disempowerment. Exploiting victim mentality involves distorting perceptions of empowerment. Individuals trapped in this mindset may perceive genuine empowerment efforts as external impositions or dismiss them as unattainable. This distortion further reinforces mental shackles by undermining the potential for personal agency and positive change.

The exploitation of victim mentality is further entrenched by feeding on negative reinforcement. Some people may seek out or unconsciously gravitate toward situations that validate their victim identity. Negative reinforcement, whether in personal relationships or external circumstances, becomes a comfort zone that sustains mental shackles by discouraging positive experiences that challenge the victim's narrative. The impact of perpetuating mental shackles through victim mentality is profound, shaping their personal narratives in ways that hinder growth, resilience, and self-actualization. A diminished sense of self-worth is a pervasive outcome, as the constant reinforcement of helplessness erodes confidence, leading them to view themselves through a lens of inadequacy. The diminished self-worth becomes a significant barrier to breaking free from mental shackles. Moreover, perpetuating mental shackles through victim mentality fosters a limited vision of possibilities. People ensnared in this mindset struggle to envision a future beyond their perceived victimhood. The prospect of personal growth, achievement, or empowerment is obscured by the overwhelming belief that change is unattainable.

Final Thoughts

Breaking free from the shackles of mental oppression demands a profound internal transformation. It necessitates a rejection of learned helplessness and the embracing of personal agency. People must confront the subtle ways in which victim mentality externalizes responsibility, fostering a culture of dependency that hinders self-sufficiency. It is a call to resist the allure of collective victimhood as a primary source of identity and to envision a future beyond the constraints of perpetual victimhood. The path to liberation involves dismantling the resistance to personal development inherent in victim mentality. It demands a rejection of self-sabotaging behaviors and a proactive engagement with opportunities for growth and improvement. Cultivating a culture of blame must be replaced with a commitment to proactive problem-solving and a recognition of the agency they hold in shaping their destinies. On a collective level, the conclusion draws attention to the manipulative external influences that exploit victim mentality for their own agendas. Whether wielded by political figures, institutions, or media, the collective victimhood of a group becomes a potent tool for those seeking to perpetuate power dynamics. Breaking free from this external manipulation necessitates a critical examination of the narratives imposed upon communities and a collective effort to redefine identities beyond the confines of victimhood.

Ultimately, there is a call for resilience, empowerment, and a reclamation of personal narratives. Breaking free from the shackles of mental oppression is not a solitary journey but a collective endeavor. It involves fostering a culture that celebrates personal agency, encourages critical self-reflection, and dismantles the subtle mechanisms that perpetuate victim mentality. The path forward is challenging, requiring a commitment to personal and collective transformation. It demands a reframing of narratives, a celebration of resilience, and an unwavering belief in the potential for positive change. In embracing this call to action, individuals and communities can embark on a journey towards liberation. A journey where the invisible chains of mental oppression are shattered, and the human spirit is free to soar toward new heights of empowerment and self-actualization. This resounding call is, IT'S PERSONAL!

Chapter Six: Breaking Free

Personal Choice

At the heart of individual agency and autonomy lies the profound concept of personal choice. It far exceeds mere decision-making, encapsulating the very essence of human freedom and responsibility. Personal choice, in its multifaceted nature, defines the trajectory of our lives, shaping our destinies through a continuous interplay of decisions, actions, and consequences. Personal choice embodies the acknowledgment that people are the architects of their own lives. It signifies a departure from a passive existence, where circumstances dictate outcomes, to an active engagement with the world. In every decision made, whether trivial or monumental, people exercise their freedom to navigate the labyrinth of life, sculpting their unique narrative with each deliberate choice. The power of personal choice lies not only in the decisions themselves but in the awareness that these choices hold the potential to transform lives. It is a celebration of human agency, an affirmation that they have the liberty to shape their circumstances, responses, and, ultimately, their destinies. This inherent freedom to choose fosters a sense of empowerment, emphasizing that each person is a conscious participant in the unfolding drama of their own existence. Furthermore, personal choice extends beyond the individual realm, resonating with societal and communal dynamics. Choices made by them contribute to the collective tapestry, weaving threads of cultural ethos and societal values. It underscores the interconnectedness of personal agency with the broader well-being of communities. The power of personal choice, when wielded responsibly, becomes a force for societal progress, influencing the cultural landscape and shaping the shared narrative.

In personal relationships, the significance of personal choice becomes particularly poignant. Every interaction, every response, is a manifestation of choice. By taking personal responsibility for these choices, people create an environment where relationships flourish. The power of choice, when exercised with thoughtfulness and intentionality, fosters open communication, mutual understanding, and the cultivation of healthy, reciprocal connections. The journey of personal choice is not immune to success and failure. However, it is within this duality that the transformative nature of personal choice reveals itself. Choices become not just a series of isolated decisions but a continuum of learning and growth. The power of personal choice is exemplified in the reflective process. Likewise, the ability to draw lessons from experiences, whether they result in triumph or setback, and to use these insights to navigate future choices more adeptly.

Personal choice serves as a compelling counterforce to the insidious grip of victim mentality and slave mentality. It stands as a declaration that individuals are not mere subjects to the whims of fate or external circumstances but active agents in their own stories. By embracing personal choice, they reject passivity in the face of challenges. Instead, they choose resilience and determination, viewing adversity as an opportunity for personal growth and self-empowerment.

Personal Responsibility

Personal responsibility is the cornerstone of self-improvement and achievement. It refers to the idea that people are accountable for their actions, choices, and behaviors, and they must take ownership of the consequences that arise from these decisions. This concept is not only essential for personal growth but also for building strong relationships and contributing positively to society. It represents a profound shift in mindset; a departure from a passive outlook on life to an active engagement with the world, recognizing the agency they possess in shaping their destinies.

The significance of personal responsibility extends beyond individual behavior, encompassing a broader commitment to contribute positively to the community and society at large. This commitment to accountability is a catalyst for personal and societal growth, fostering resilience, promoting accountability, and driving continuous self-improvement. Taking personal responsibility means acknowledging that your life outcomes are largely influenced by your choices. This mindset empowers them to make informed choices. By recognizing that choices have consequences, one becomes more mindful of decisions and seeks information, evaluates options, and makes choices that align with one's aspirations and ethics.

Learning and adapting to embrace personal responsibilities allows learning from mistakes and failures and is inherently empowering. In contrast to blaming external factors, assess the failures and use that knowledge to improve and grow. It grants people the agency to be architects of their own destinies, steering their lives toward meaningful outcomes. It emphasizes the freedom to make choices and the understanding that these choices contribute to the unfolding narrative of our lives. This freedom, when coupled with a sense of responsibility, becomes a potent force for personal and collective well-being. In turn, this will foster a sense of accountability. Personal responsibility encourages one to hold oneself accountable for commitments and obligations. Whether it's meeting deadlines at work or honoring promises to friends and family, take these responsibilities seriously.

One of the profound aspects of personal responsibility is its role in building resilience. Those who actively take responsibility for their actions are better equipped to navigate challenges, setbacks, and failures. Rather than viewing adversity as insurmountable and giving in to defeat, individuals see it as an opportunity for growth, learning, and adaptation. The acknowledgment of personal responsibility becomes a cornerstone for developing the mental fortitude needed to face life's uncertainties. Furthermore, personal responsibility fosters a culture of accountability. When they acknowledge their role in the outcomes of their lives, they contribute to a society where accountability is valued. This accountability extends to relationships, work environments, and societal structures, creating a foundation for trust and cooperation. The interconnectedness of personal responsibility and accountability serves as a cornerstone for healthy relationships and collaborative endeavors.

In personal relationships, a commitment to personal responsibility strengthens the bonds between people. Taking ownership of one's actions promotes open communication, conflict resolution, and mutual understanding. It creates an environment where trust can flourish, and relationships can evolve towards greater intimacy and connection. By embodying personal responsibility, they contribute to the creation of meaningful, reciprocal relationships that enhance the fabric of social connections. Embracing personal responsibility is also a catalyst for personal growth. Those who actively seek self-improvement set meaningful goals, and work towards them with dedication experience continuous development. The recognition that personal growth is a lifelong journey contributes to a sense of purpose and fulfillment. This commitment to growth extends beyond personal benefit, influencing the broader community through the positive example set by those who embody personal responsibility. A society built on personal responsibility is one where people actively contribute to the collective well-being. Recognizing the impact of their actions on the broader community, responsible citizens engage in activities that promote social harmony, justice, and progress. This collective responsibility is fundamental for the flourishing of societies, as it builds a foundation of shared values and mutual respect.

Ultimately, personal responsibility is a key driver of success. Whether in education, career, or personal life, those who take ownership of their actions are more likely to achieve their goals. However, personal responsibility does not mean you should ignore external factors that influence your life. It acknowledges that while external circumstances can impact your journey, your response and decisions are what truly matter. It's about proactively shaping your destiny rather than being a passive observer.

Personal Growth

Personal growth is a profound trek that transcends the mundane and becomes a transformative exploration of self-discovery, resilience, and continual improvement. Rooted in the inherent human desire for evolution and self-realization, personal growth is a dynamic process that unfolds across the diverse landscapes of our lives. At its core, personal growth is a testament to the human capacity for change and adaptation. It is an acknowledgment that, as individuals, we are not static entities but rather dynamic beings with the potential for continuous development. This journey of growth encompasses various dimensions, including emotional, intellectual, spiritual, and interpersonal facets, weaving a rich tapestry that reflects the complexity of the human experience.

One of the fundamental aspects of personal growth lies in the cultivation of self-awareness. It is the ability to introspect, to delve into the depths of one's thoughts, emotions, and behaviors. This self-awareness becomes the compass guiding the journey of growth, illuminating the areas that require attention, nurturing, and transformation. Through introspection, people gain insights into their strengths, weaknesses, and the underlying patterns that shape their lives. The path of personal growth is often intertwined with the development of resilience. Life is replete with challenges, setbacks, and unforeseen circumstances. Personal growth involves not only weathering these storms but also using them as catalysts for transformation. It is the ability to bounce back from adversity, to find meaning in the face of hardship, and to emerge stronger and more resilient than before. In navigating the turbulent waters of life, they discover the depths of their inner strength and the capacity to endure.

Additionally, personal growth is deeply rooted in the pursuit of knowledge and intellectual expansion. It involves a commitment to lifelong learning and a hunger for understanding the world and oneself. This intellectual growth transcends formal education; it is a continuous curiosity that propels people to seek knowledge from diverse sources, question assumptions, and embrace the ever-evolving nature of human understanding. The pursuit of knowledge becomes a catalyst for personal empowerment, broadening perspectives and fostering a deeper understanding of the interconnectedness of all things. The journey of personal growth extends to the emotional realm, encompassing the development of emotional intelligence and well-being. It involves an exploration of one's emotional landscape and an understanding of the myriad feelings that color our experiences. Emotional growth is marked by an ability to manage and regulate emotions, to empathize with others, and to forge meaningful connections. As they grow emotionally, they cultivate a sense of emotional resilience that equips them to navigate the complexities of relationships and navigate the ebb and flow of life's emotional currents.

Furthermore, personal growth involves a spiritual dimension, irrespective of religious affiliations. It is a quest for meaning, purpose, and a connection to something greater than oneself. Spiritual growth is an inward journey, a reflection on the profound questions of existence and the cultivation of a sense of inner peace. This dimension of personal growth is deeply personal and often involves practices such as mindfulness, meditation, or a quest for deeper philosophical understanding.

Interpersonal growth is also a fundamental aspect of the journey, as people navigate the intricacies of relationships and connections with others. It involves the development of effective communication skills, empathy, and the ability to collaborate and build meaningful connections. Interpersonal growth fosters an awareness of the impact of one's actions on others, promoting healthy relationships and contributing to the fabric of social harmony.

The journey of personal growth is not without its challenges. It requires a willingness to step out of comfort zones, to confront fears and uncertainties, and to embrace change. Growth often involves letting go of ingrained patterns and belief systems that may no longer serve one's evolution. This process of shedding old layers, while liberating, can be daunting, requiring courage and a commitment to personal authenticity. In essence, personal growth is a transformative journey that unfolds across the entirety of one's life. It is not a destination but a continual process of becoming. The seeds of growth are sown in self-awareness, nurtured through resilience, and cultivated through a commitment to lifelong learning and introspection. As individuals embark on this journey, they discover the profound beauty of human potential, the resilience of the human spirit, and the capacity for continual reinvention. The impact of personal growth extends far beyond the individual. It ripples outward, influencing relationships, communities, and the broader society. Those who embark on a journey of personal growth become beacons of inspiration, embodying the transformative power of intentional evolution. Their stories become testaments to the human capacity for change, resilience, and the continual pursuit of a more authentic and fulfilling life.

Personal Failure

Failure is often regarded as a daunting and disheartening aspect of life but it also has within its folds the potential for profound transformation and personal growth. Personal responsibility and personal failure are interconnected aspects of life. It is an inevitable companion on the journey of self-discovery, a mirror reflecting the complexities of the human experience. In examining personal failure, one encounters not just the sting of disappointment but also the seeds of resilience, learning, and a resilient spirit that can lead to unparalleled personal development.

Personal responsibility means acknowledging that we are accountable for our actions and decisions. When we encounter personal failure, it signifies that our choices or actions did not yield the desired outcome. It's essential to understand that personal responsibility doesn't mean avoiding failure, but rather facing it with maturity and resilience because failure is an inherent and inescapable facet of life. Failure is a reality that, when embraced with personal responsibility, can transform into a pivotal stepping stone towards eventual success. It is a universal experience that transcends societal boundaries, demanding recognition not as a permanent setback but as an indispensable chapter in the narrative of personal and professional growth. The crucial element lies in the individual's capacity to take ownership of their actions and decisions, to engage in self-reflection, and to actively pursue avenues of improvement. This reflective process, prompted by failure, serves as a crucible for the development of resilience, a trait that enables them to navigate challenges with fortitude and adaptability. The commitment to continuous self-improvement becomes the driving force, propelling one forward on a path of learning and evolution. As failures accumulate and are met with personal responsibility, they contribute to the construction of wisdom and strength. Wisdom arises from the assimilation of knowledge gleaned from experiences, while strength is forged through the crucible of resilience and perseverance. Ultimately, this consolidation of lessons learned, personal growth, and an unwavering commitment to overcoming challenges culminate in the realization of achievement. Success, therefore, emerges not as a stroke of luck but as the tangible outcome of a journey marked by the transformative power of failure coupled with personal responsibility.

In The Context of The Slave Mentality...

Within the framework of the victim mentality, personal responsibility emerges as a vital counterforce, offering a transformative perspective that contrasts with the perceived helplessness inherent in the victim mindset. The slave mentality manifests as a cognitive pattern where individuals attribute their challenges exclusively to external forces, often avoiding self-examination and personal accountability. In stark contrast, personal responsibility serves as a catalyst for change, challenging them to cultivate self-awareness and reclaim a sense of empowerment over their lives.

At its core, personal responsibility prompts people to confront and dismantle the slave mentality by fostering a deep understanding of their own agency in shaping their circumstances. Even when external factors play a role, taking personal responsibility involves a courageous acknowledgment of one's own contributions to the situation. This mindset reframes the narrative, directing attention away from external circumstances and towards an active exploration of what can be done to improve one's own conditions.

Owning one's actions and choices becomes a cornerstone of personal responsibility. It involves a mature acceptance of accountability, recognizing that personal decisions play a crucial role in shaping outcomes. This acceptance is not a form of self-blame but rather a powerful acknowledgment that, even in the face of adversity, individuals can exert influence through intentional decision-making. Moreover, personal responsibility empowers them to view challenges as opportunities for growth rather than insurmountable obstacles. This mindset encourages a proactive approach to problem-solving, where they actively seek solutions and learn from their experiences. By embracing personal responsibility, they break free from the cycle of negativity and disempowerment associated with the victim mentality.

In essence, personal responsibility serves as a potent tool for transcending the victim mentality. It becomes a catalyst for self-improvement, fostering positive relationships, and facilitating the pursuit of personal and professional goals. By instilling a sense of agency and control, personal responsibility empowers people to navigate challenges with resilience, ultimately leading to a more constructive and fulfilling life.

Breaking The Chains

Breaking mental chains through personal responsibility and personal choice is a profound journey of self-liberation, where people actively engage in shaping their own destinies. This transformative process hinges on the recognition that, despite external circumstances and influences, they possess the autonomy to make choices and take responsibility for their own lives. At the core of breaking mental chains lies the acknowledgment that they are the architects of their own mental landscapes. It involves a deliberate and conscious effort to take ownership of one's thoughts, beliefs, and actions. By assuming responsibility for the direction of their lives, they break free from the shackles of external influences and societal expectations that may have contributed to limiting mindsets. Personal responsibility, in the context of mental liberation, entails a rigorous examination of one's choices and their consequences. This self-awareness enables them to identify patterns of thinking or behavior that may be contributing to the mental chains they seek to break. By understanding the power of personal choice, they can actively steer away from negative thought patterns, consciously choosing thoughts and actions that align with their values and aspirations.

Personal choice emerges as a catalyst for breaking mental chains when individuals recognize the agency they possess in shaping their own narratives. It involves making intentional decisions that reflect one's values, desires, and goals. The recognition that every choice, no matter how small, contributes to the overall trajectory of one's life empowers them to break free from the notion of being passive recipients of their circumstances.

Moreover, personal choice allows people to redefine their perspectives and beliefs. It involves actively selecting empowering narratives that align with personal growth and resilience. By choosing to focus on positive aspects of life and possibilities for change, they shift their mental framework, breaking free from the constraints of self-limiting beliefs that may have been imposed by external influences.

Breaking mental chains through personal responsibility and personal choice also necessitates a commitment to continuous learning and growth. It involves actively seeking knowledge, challenging preconceived notions, and being open to new possibilities. This commitment to growth empowers people to evolve beyond the mental constraints of past experiences and societal conditioning.

Final Thoughts

Personal responsibility is foundational to individual empowerment, providing a framework for taking charge of one's life. This mindset involves making informed choices, navigating challenges with resilience, and fostering personal growth. By embracing personal responsibility, people cultivate a sense of agency, enabling them to forge meaningful relationships and work towards goals with determination. It acts as a powerful tool, propelling them towards success and fulfillment, emphasizing the transformative impact of proactive decision-making and accountability in shaping a purpose-driven and empowered life.

The assertion that personal choice serves as a potent antidote to the victim mentality underscores the transformative influence that conscious decision-making holds. When people actively engage in utilizing their personal agency, they reclaim control over their lives, disrupting the pervasive sense of powerlessness associated with victimhood. Personal choice becomes a catalyst for empowerment, offering a pathway out of the cyclic narrative of helplessness. By embracing personal choice, one not only acknowledges the capacity to make decisions but also recognizes the inherent ability to shape the trajectory of one's life. This shift from a passive victim mindset to an active participant in decision-making instills a sense of autonomy and self-determination. Proactive choices, aligned with personal values and aspirations, stand as a declaration of independence from the constraints of victimhood.

In essence, the journey of breaking mental chains through personal responsibility and personal choice is a dynamic process of self-empowerment. It requires active engagement with thoughts, beliefs, and actions, recognizing the transformative potential of every choice made. By assuming responsibility for one's life and making intentional choices that align with personal values and aspirations, one liberates oneself from mental chains, paving the way for a more empowered, purposeful, and fulfilling existence.

Chapter Seven: A Path to Empowerment and Liberation

Cultivate Self-Awareness

Cultivating self-awareness is a profound and transformative journey that involves a multifaceted exploration of one's emotional, mental, and behavioral landscape. At its core, self-awareness is the ability to recognize and understand one's own emotions. This foundational element lays the groundwork for emotional regulation, resilience, and a deeper connection to the inner self. The journey toward self-awareness is not a linear path but rather a dynamic process that unfolds over time, requiring introspection, self-reflection, and a commitment to personal growth.

One crucial aspect of cultivating self-awareness is the practice of emotional self-awareness. This involves developing the ability to identify, understand, and express emotions in a healthy and constructive way. Emotions serve as powerful signals, providing valuable insights into our needs, desires, and reactions to various situations. Through self-awareness, one can gain a nuanced understanding of one's emotional landscape, distinguishing between different emotions and recognizing the underlying causes. Moreover, emotional self-awareness extends beyond merely recognizing emotions to the skill of emotional regulation. People with a high level of self-awareness can navigate their emotional terrain with greater ease, regulating their emotions in response to external stimuli. This capacity for emotional regulation not only contributes to mental well-being but also enhances interpersonal relationships by fostering empathy and effective communication.

A cornerstone of cultivating self-awareness is the practice of reflective thinking. Regular reflection, whether through journaling, meditation, or other contemplative practices, provides the opportunity to explore thoughts, feelings, and behaviors. It allows for a deeper understanding of the factors influencing one's decisions and actions. Through reflection, people can unravel patterns of behavior, identify recurring themes in their lives, and gain insights from past experiences.

Reflective thinking also involves questioning and examining one's core values and beliefs. Understanding these fundamental aspects of the self is essential for living authentically and aligning actions with personal values. This self-awareness helps people make choices that resonate with their authentic selves, fostering a sense of purpose and fulfillment. The journey toward self-awareness is not isolated to one's internal world, it extends to interactions with others. Social awareness is a key dimension of self-awareness, involving an understanding of how one's actions and words impact those around them. This heightened awareness of social dynamics contributes to the development of the ability to understand and share the feelings of others. Empathy plays a very pivotal role in building and maintaining meaningful relationships. By being attuned to the emotions and perspectives of others, People who are self-aware can navigate social interactions with sensitivity and understanding. This interpersonal skill enhances communication, fosters collaboration, and contributes to the creation of a supportive and empathetic social environment.

Setting and achieving meaningful goals is another area where self-awareness comes into play as well as the concept of mindfulness. People who have a deep understanding of their strengths and weaknesses are better equipped to set realistic and purposeful goals. This self-awareness allows for the alignment of personal aspirations with one's capabilities, increasing the likelihood of success and fulfillment. Self-awareness is closely tied to a state of heightened awareness and presence in the current moment. Mindfulness practices, such as meditation and mindful breathing, are powerful tools for cultivating self-awareness. These practices encourage people to observe their thoughts and emotions without judgment, fostering a non-reactive and non-impulsive mindset. By living in the present moment, one can break free from the burdens of the past and anxieties about the future, promoting a sense of calm and clarity.

Personal accountability and proactive problem-solving are also integral aspects of self-awareness. Acknowledging and taking responsibility for one's actions is a hallmark of self-aware individuals. This accountability is rooted in an honest assessment of one's choices, behaviors, and their impact on oneself and others. By accepting accountability, individuals can learn from their mistakes, make amends when necessary, and actively participate in their own personal growth. Proactive problem-solving is a natural outcome of self-awareness. Rather than reacting impulsively to challenges, self-aware individuals approach problems with a thoughtful and deliberate mindset. They draw upon their understanding of their strengths and weaknesses, leverage their emotional intelligence, and seek creative and effective solutions. This proactive approach enhances problem-solving skills and contributes to a sense of empowerment and self-efficacy.

The journey of self-awareness is not a destination but an ongoing process of growth and self-discovery. It involves a commitment to lifelong learning and a willingness to adapt and evolve. Embracing a growth mindset allows people to view challenges as opportunities for learning and personal development. This proactive approach to self-awareness fosters resilience in the face of adversity and promotes a positive and optimistic outlook on life.

Challenge Internalized Beliefs

Breaking free from slave mentality requires challenging internalized beliefs that perpetuate feelings of inferiority, powerlessness, and dependency. This involves critically examining the narratives that have been ingrained over time and consciously choosing to reject limiting beliefs. Affirmative action, positive self-talk, and the cultivation of a growth mindset are essential tools in this process. By challenging negative self-perceptions and fostering a sense of self-efficacy, people can disrupt the mental chains that anchor them to a mindset of subservience.

Central to this journey is the critical examination of the narratives that have been absorbed, often unconsciously, over the course of one's life. These narratives may have originated from societal stereotypes, cultural expectations, or personal experiences that contribute to a distorted self-perception. By shining a light on these ingrained beliefs, one gains the power to consciously challenge and dismantle them. This process involves questioning the validity of limiting beliefs, recognizing their origins, and acknowledging that they do not define one's inherent worth or potential.

Affirmative action, positive self-talk, and cultivating a growth mindset emerge as powerful tools for breaking free from a slave mentality. By actively and intentionally choosing positive actions that affirm one's capabilities and worth, individuals can disrupt the ingrained patterns of self-doubt and negativity. This might involve setting and achieving small goals, celebrating personal accomplishments, and surrounding oneself with positive influences that reinforce a healthier self-perception. Affirmative action serves as a tangible manifestation of the internal shift, fostering a sense of agency and control over one's own narrative. Equally, the language we use internally shapes our perception of ourselves and the world around us. By consciously replacing negative self-talk with affirming and empowering language, individuals can rewire their thought patterns. This shift not only enhances self-esteem but also contributes to the cultivation of a more resilient and optimistic mindset. Positive self-talk becomes a daily practice of self-empowerment, serving as a continuous reminder that individuals have the agency to shape their own narratives. Instead of viewing abilities and intelligence as fixed traits, a growth mindset sees them as qualities that can be cultivated and expanded through effort and perseverance. Embracing a growth mindset encourages individuals to see challenges as opportunities for learning and growth, rather than insurmountable obstacles. This shift in perspective is fundamental to breaking free from the shackles of a slave mentality, as it opens the door to possibilities and reinforces the idea that individuals can shape their destinies.

Disrupting mental chains requires a holistic approach that encompasses both individual and collective efforts. Building a supportive community and seeking allies in the journey toward mental liberation can provide invaluable encouragement and reinforcement. Sharing experiences, insights, and strategies with others who are on a similar path fosters a sense of solidarity and mutual empowerment. Breaking free from a slave mentality demands, however, a deliberate and transformative process of challenging internalized beliefs, critically examining ingrained narratives, and consciously choosing affirmative actions. Affirmative action, positive self-talk, and the cultivation of a growth mindset serve as essential tools in disrupting the mental chains that anchor individuals to feelings of inferiority, powerlessness, and dependency. This journey is not only an individual endeavor but also a collective effort that thrives on shared experiences, support, and the collective realization that every individual possesses the inherent agency to shape their own narrative and break free from the constraints of a limiting mindset.

Education and Knowledge Empowerment

Education plays a pivotal role in dismantling the mental chains of the slave mentality. Empowering oneself with knowledge about history, culture, and the complexities of systemic oppression provides a foundation for understanding the roots of slave mentality. Learning about the resilience and achievements of marginalized communities throughout history can serve as a source of inspiration and empowerment. Education becomes a tool for redefining personal identity and fostering a sense of pride in one's heritage, countering the historical narratives that perpetuate a sense of inferiority. It is one of the most powerful tools for disentangling the intricacies of the perception or reality of systemic oppression. It illuminates the historical context that has shaped the narratives of marginalized communities. The ability to differentiate facts from follies is an epically important step in unlocking the mental chains.

Moreover, education serves as a catalyst for the redefinition of personal identity. As individuals deepen their understanding of their cultural heritage and the challenges faced by their ancestors, they gain a profound sense of connection to a broader narrative. The knowledge acquired becomes a foundation upon which individuals can build a stronger sense of self, fostering a deep-seated pride in their heritage. This pride becomes a potent antidote to the historical narratives that have perpetuated a sense of inferiority and inadequacy.

The transformative power of education lies not only in the acquisition of facts and figures but in the cultivation of critical thinking skills. It encourages individuals to question existing narratives, to challenge the status quo, and to engage with diverse perspectives. This critical engagement with information is essential in dismantling the mental chains of a slave mentality, as it enables individuals to discern between truth and distortion, reality, and myth. Education, therefore, becomes a tool for liberation, empowering individuals to think independently and construct their own narratives.

The process of education in dismantling a slave mentality is not without its challenges. It requires a commitment to unlearning ingrained biases and confronting uncomfortable truths. Through the acquisition of knowledge about history, culture, and systemic oppression, individuals gain a foundation for understanding the roots of their own struggles. Learning about the triumphs of marginalized communities becomes a source of inspiration and empowerment, challenging the narratives of inferiority. Education serves as a tool for redefining personal identity and fostering pride in one's heritage, counteracting the historical narratives that have sought to diminish worth.

The impact of education extends to the collective consciousness of communities as well. A well-informed and educated community is better equipped to advocate for justice, equality, and systemic change. Education fosters a collective awareness of systemic issues and provides the tools necessary for community members to engage in meaningful dialogue and action. In this way, education becomes a driving force for societal transformation, breaking the cycle of generational ignorance and challenging the structures that perpetuate inequality.

Community Building and Collective Healing

Breaking free from the mental chains of slave mentality is not an isolated journey; it is a collective endeavor. Communities affected by historical injustices must come together to share experiences, validate each other's struggles, and collectively heal. Creating safe spaces for dialogue and mutual support facilitates the exchange of stories and strategies for overcoming shared challenges. Through community building, people can draw strength from their collective history and experiences, reinforcing a sense of solidarity that counteracts the isolation perpetuated by the slave mentality.

Community building, in this context, extends beyond the sharing of stories and strategies; it involves drawing strength from a collective history and shared experiences. By recognizing the resilience of their community throughout history, individuals gain a profound source of inspiration. The communal narrative becomes a testament to the strength, endurance, and capacity for transformation inherent in the community. This collective history serves as a counter-narrative to the oppressive ideologies that have sought to undermine the worth and potential of the community. It reinforces a sense of solidarity, creating a network of support that extends beyond individual experiences. Individuals within the community are no longer isolated in their struggles; they are part of a larger tapestry of resilience and resistance. This collective identity becomes a powerful antidote to the divisive tactics employed by the slave mentality, which seeks to fragment and weaken the bonds of communities.

Cultural Reclamation and Celebration

Cultural reclamation is a powerful tool in breaking the mental chains of the slave mentality. Celebrating cultural heritage, traditions, and achievements fosters a sense of pride and identity that challenges narratives of inferiority. Embracing cultural practices, languages, and customs becomes a form of resistance against historical erasure and an affirmation of the richness and resilience of marginalized communities. Cultural reclamation provides a platform for people to define themselves on their terms, outside the confines of fallacious narratives.

Cultural reclamation is not just a retrospective endeavor but a forward-looking affirmation of identity. It serves as a living testimony to the endurance and resilience of marginalized communities, showcasing their ability to thrive in the face of adversity. Through the active celebration of achievements and traditions, individuals lay claim to a narrative of strength, creativity, and innovation that counters historical attempts to portray them as passive victims. It also provides a vital platform for individuals to define themselves on their terms. In a world often dominated by external perceptions and stereotypes, this act of self-definition becomes a critical aspect of personal empowerment. It allows individuals to transcend the limiting narratives imposed upon them, providing a space where they can authentically express their multifaceted identities. This act of self-definition is not only liberating on an individual level but also contributes to reshaping broader societal perceptions, challenging stereotypes, and fostering a more inclusive understanding of diverse cultures.

The act of celebrating cultural heritage serves as a sensitive counter-narrative, challenging the historical ideologies that sought to diminish the worth and potential of specific communities. Through this celebration, individuals actively reject the imposed narrative of inferiority, instead choosing to highlight the numerous contributions, innovations, and traditions that have shaped their cultural bond. This intentional focus on the positive aspects of cultural identity becomes a source of strength and resilience, fostering a collective consciousness that empowers individuals to redefine themselves beyond the constraints of oppressive historical narratives. Embracing, practicing, and keeping alive cultural practices, languages, and customs becomes a form of resistance, signaling a refusal to succumb to historical erasure. Often, throughout history, marginalized communities have experienced attempts to erase, dilute, alter, or even substitute their cultural identities as part of broader progressive agendas. Cultural reclamation, however, provides a means of resisting by actively engaging with and revitalizing these elements. Language, in particular, plays a crucial role, as it serves as a carrier of cultural identity and a repository of collective memory. By preserving and revitalizing indigenous languages, for example, communities assert their resistance to the linguistic assimilation that has historically been a tool for integration.

Mindfulness and Mental Resilience Practices

Mindfulness practices, such as meditation and self-reflection, can be instrumental in breaking the mental chains of slave mentality. By cultivating present-moment awareness, people can detach themselves from the negative narratives that may have become deeply internalized over time. Incorporating mindfulness practices into daily life contributes to a positive mental shift, empowering people to break free from the cyclical patterns of negative thinking.

One of the profound impacts of mindfulness is its role in fostering mental resilience. In the face of historical traumas and the weight of oppressive narratives, individuals may find themselves grappling with emotional and psychological challenges. Mindfulness, through its emphasis on being fully present in the moment, equips individuals with a heightened capacity to navigate these challenges. By developing an awareness of their thoughts and emotions, individuals can respond to them with greater insight and objectivity. This enhanced resilience is particularly crucial in breaking free from the cyclical patterns of negative thinking that often characterize a slave mentality.

Mindfulness contributes significantly to emotional regulation, a crucial skill in the quest for liberation from a slave mentality. Emotions are often deeply intertwined with historical traumas and internalized narratives. Mindfulness provides individuals with the tools to observe their emotional responses without being overwhelmed by them. This cultivated emotional awareness empowers individuals to respond to challenges with a balanced and measured approach, reducing the likelihood of being entangled in reactive patterns rooted in historical wounds. By incorporating mindfulness practices into daily life, it becomes a continuous process of self-discovery and empowerment.

Mindfulness serves as a constant companion, guiding people in their journey to break free from the shackles of a slave mentality. By fostering present-moment awareness, individuals develop an anchor that allows them to stay rooted in the now, reducing the influence of historical narratives that might otherwise overshadow their sense of self.

Along with meditation and self-reflection, mindfulness practices offer a profound and transformative means of breaking the mental chains associated with a slave mentality. By cultivating present-moment awareness, individuals gain the capacity to distance themselves from negative internalized narratives. Mindfulness becomes a beacon of clarity, developing mental resilience and providing individuals with the tools to navigate emotional challenges with insight and objectivity. The incorporation of mindfulness into daily life facilitates a positive mental shift, empowering individuals to break free from cyclical patterns of negative thinking and encouraging a continuous journey of self-discovery and empowerment.

Empowerment through Economic and Political Engagement

Economic and political empowerment stands as a potent and multifaceted approach to breaking free from the mental chains of a slave mentality. Actively engaging in economic endeavors, entrepreneurship, and political participation becomes a means of reclaiming agency and challenging systemic inequalities that may have historically confined certain communities. By entering the economic sphere, individuals not only secure financial independence but also play a crucial role in reshaping their narrative within society. Entrepreneurship, in particular, becomes a powerful tool for individuals to establish their ventures, contribute to economic growth, and assert their capabilities in the face of historical narratives that may have perpetuated a sense of powerlessness.

Participation in political processes is equally pivotal in the journey to break free from the mental chains associated with a slave mentality. Political engagement allows individuals to become active contributors to the shaping of policies and institutions that have a profound impact on their lives. Through active involvement in the political sphere, individuals can challenge and transform systemic inequalities that have historically marginalized certain communities. This engagement goes beyond mere participation; it becomes a vehicle for advocacy, representation, and the dismantling of structures that perpetuate a sense of powerlessness. By actively shaping political landscapes, individuals can redefine their roles in society, affirming their presence, and challenging historical narratives that may have sought to relegate them to the margins.

Moreover, economic and political empowerment intertwine, creating a symbiotic relationship that reinforces the journey to break mental chains. Economic empowerment provides individuals with the means to access education, healthcare, and various opportunities that can further bolster their political engagement. Simultaneously, political empowerment offers individuals the agency to shape economic policies and structures that foster inclusivity and equality. The interaction between economic and political empowerment becomes a powerful force in dismantling mental chains, as individuals move from passive recipients of systemic forces to active participants in shaping their destinies.

Final Thoughts

Slave mentality, a psychological framework deeply rooted in the historical subjugation and dehumanization of almost every society, casts a long shadow over individuals and communities today. Its origins lie in the brutal history of slavery, where systemic abuse, denying human dignity or dignity to others, making them seem less than others, and the stripping away of basic human rights left an indelible mark on the psyche of those subjected to such inhumane treatment. Breaking free from this mental captivity is a complex and nuanced process that requires a combination of individual self-awareness, collective action, and a profound redefinition of personal and communal narratives.

Self-awareness serves as a foundational step in dismantling the mental chains of a slave mentality. It involves a deep and introspective understanding of one's own thoughts, beliefs, and behaviors, particularly those influenced by historical trauma. Through self-reflection and examination, one can identify the internalized narratives and negative thought patterns that perpetuate the slave mentality. This process demands a courageous confrontation with the painful remnants of historical oppression and a commitment to healing. It is through self-awareness that individuals can reclaim agency over their thoughts and perceptions, gradually unraveling the layers of internalized oppression and fostering a renewed sense of self.

Redefining personal and communal narratives forms the root of the journey toward breaking free from a slave mentality. It involves a conscious effort to reshape the stories that have been historically imposed upon individuals and communities. By celebrating cultural heritage, achievements, and resilience, individuals contribute to a counter-narrative that challenges the historical ideologies of inferiority. This redefinition is not a denial of history but a reclaiming of agency over the narrative, allowing individuals and communities to shape their identities beyond the constraints of historical narratives. Through the deliberate reconstruction of personal and communal stories, individuals find the power to redefine their roles in society, asserting their worth and potential in a way that transcends the mental captivity of a slave mentality.

Breaking the mental chains of slave mentality is a profound journey that demands an elevated level of self-awareness, communal action, and a commitment to reshaping personal and collective narratives. By cultivating self-awareness, challenging internalized beliefs, embracing education, building resilient communities, reclaiming cultural identity, practicing mindfulness, and engaging in economic and political empowerment, one can forge a path towards liberation. The process requires dedication, patience, a continuous commitment to self-discovery, growth, and perseverance to follow through until the end. As people break free from their mental chains, they pave the way for a more empowered and liberated future, not only for themselves but for generations to come.

Epilogue/Conclusion

The transition from mental slavery to breaking free from mental chains is a profound and transformative journey, marked by self-discovery, resilience, and a courageous confrontation with historical trauma. Mental slavery, rooted in the historical oppression and dehumanization of certain communities, manifests as a deeply ingrained psychological framework that influences thoughts, beliefs, and behaviors. This oppressive mindset casts a long shadow, shaping individual and collective narratives and perpetuating a sense of powerlessness. The process of breaking free from these mental chains involves self-awareness, collective action, and a radical redefinition of personal and communal narratives.

At the heart of this transition is self-awareness—an intimate exploration of one's own psyche to unravel the layers of internalized oppression. Individuals must confront the negative thought patterns and beliefs that have been ingrained through historical trauma. This process requires courage and a willingness to delve into the painful remnants of the past. Through self-reflection, individuals can identify the subtle ways in which mental slavery has influenced their perceptions of self and others. It is a journey of reclaiming agency over one's thoughts, untangling the complex web of internalized narratives, and fostering a renewed sense of self.

Collective action stands as a pillar in the transition from mental slavery to liberation. Communities affected by historical injustices must unite in a shared effort to challenge and transform the systemic structures that perpetuate mental captivity. Open dialogue, mutual support, and the sharing of experiences become essential components of this collective journey. By collectively acknowledging the impact of historical trauma, communities can break the isolation perpetuated by the slave mentality. Activism and community organizing serve as powerful tools to challenge systemic inequalities and advocate for change. The strength of collective action lies in its ability to foster resilience, solidarity, and a shared commitment to rewriting narratives that have confined communities to a legacy of oppression.

Redefining personal and communal narratives is a transformative act that solidifies the transition from mental slavery to breaking free from mental chains. It involves a conscious effort to reshape the stories historically imposed upon individuals and communities. By celebrating cultural heritage, achievements, and resilience, individuals contribute to a counter-narrative that challenges historical ideologies of inferiority. This redefinition is not a denial of history but a reclaiming of agency over the narrative. It allows individuals and communities to shape their identities beyond the constraints of oppressive historical narratives. Through the deliberate reconstruction of personal and communal stories, individuals find the power to redefine their roles in society, asserting their worth and potential in a way that transcends the mental captivity of a slave mentality.

The transition from mental slavery to breaking free from mental chains is a dynamic and holistic process that demands inner introspection and outward collective action. It requires individuals to confront their internalized oppression, communities to unite in challenging systemic inequalities, and a profound redefinition of personal and communal narratives. Through this journey, individuals emerge with a renewed sense of agency, resilience, and empowerment. Breaking free from mental chains becomes an act of liberation, not only from historical trauma but also from the enduring impacts of oppressive mindsets. It paves the way for a future where individuals and communities can thrive beyond the limitations imposed by mental slavery, forging a path toward a more just and liberated existence. Victim mentality is a psychological mindset where people habitually perceive themselves as perpetual victims of external circumstances, often to an exaggerated or unjustified extent. This mindset is characterized by a belief that external forces, such as other people, societal systems, or fate, bear the primary responsibility for one's problems and hardships. In essence, those with a victim mentality tend to deflect personal responsibility and instead attribute their difficulties exclusively to external factors. This way of thinking can be detrimental to personal growth, relationships, and overall well-being.

Prior to writing this book I strongly believed that one of the key aspects of the victim mentality is external attributions. Those trapped in this mindset customarily assign the blame for their challenges to external factors. Instead of examining their own actions or choices, they point fingers at others, societal structures, or circumstances beyond their control. This pattern of external attribution can lead to a sense of powerlessness and inaction, as one comes to believe they have little control over one's own life. Those with this mindset often see themselves as helpless victims, believing they lack the agency or capacity to change their circumstances. They may become resigned to their situations and abandon efforts to improve their lives, as they feel that external forces are insurmountable.

Chronic negativity and self-pity are two other very common features of the victim mentality. Those who share these two mindsets tend to focus on perceived injustices, reliving past grievances and often dwelling on the negative aspects of their lives. They may constantly recount their hardships and grievances to gain attention and support, perpetuating a cycle of self-pity that can alienate those around them. This negativity can lead to feelings of bitterness, anger, and resentment, which not only affect their mental health but also strain their relationships with others.

In my opinion, the worst feature of them all is avoidance of personal responsibility is central to the victim mentality. These people may shirk accountability for their choices and actions, preferring to cast themselves as passive victims of their own lives. This avoidance of responsibility tends to impede personal growth and development, as it inhibits self-reflection and learning from one's mistakes.

Countering the victim mindset with personal responsibility is a transformative journey toward empowerment and self-growth. The victim mindset, marked by a belief in external forces dictating one's life and avoiding personal accountability, can be debilitating. However, I strongly believe that personal responsibility offers one of, if not the best, path to break free from this negative pattern. By embracing personal responsibility, one has to first acknowledge one's own role when circumstances arise. This self-awareness is pivotal in challenging victimhood. It empowers people to recognize that they possess agency and control over their lives, enabling them to shift from feeling powerless to becoming proactive agents of change.

Taking personal responsibility involves accepting accountability for one's actions and choices, especially in challenging situations. It encourages people to understand that while external factors may influence some outcomes, their decisions and responses play an even more crucial role. This shift in perspective fosters resilience as challenges are viewed as opportunities for growth and learning.

Ultimately, countering the victim mindset with personal responsibility is a journey toward personal development, goal achievement, and a more positive outlook on life. It empowers everyone to take control of their destinies, face challenges head-on, and work towards a future that they actively shape.

Personal Responsibility opens the door to learning, which is paramount for Education, which opens the door to the world!!

Bibliography

Barry, B. (1997). The slave trade in the eighteenth century. In *Senegambia and the Atlantic Slave Trade* (African Studies, pp. 61-80). Cambridge: Cambridge University Press. doi:10.1017/CBO9780511584084.009

The Human Origin Project. The First Civilization on Earth: Sumerians from Ancient Mesopotamia. Retrieved from https://humanoriginproject.com/first-civilization-earth-sumerians-ancient-mesopotamia/

Little, Becky (2019) After Charles I of Spain signed an edict allowing slave ships to travel directly from Africa to the Americas, human cargo on transatlantic voyages spiked nearly tenfold. *Details of Brutal First Slave Voyages Discovered*. Retrieved from https://www.history.com/news/transatlantic-slave-first-ships-details

Ceesay, H. and Green, T. (n.d.) Trans-Saharan Trade. Origins, organization, and effects in the development of West Africa. *West African Senior School Certificate Examination*. Retrieved from https://wasscehistorytextbook.com/2-trans-saharan-trade-origins-organization-and-effects-in-the-development-of-west-africa/

(n.d.) HISTORY OF SLAVERY. *Historyworld*. Retrieved from http://www.historyworld.net/wrldhis/PlainTextHistories.asp?historyid=ac41

(January 1, 2016) The Untold Story Of White Slavery (Ottoman Turks, Arab, And Barbary Muslim Slave Trade). *SLAVIC WORLD*. Retrieved from https://archive.org/details/
TheUntoldStoryOfWhiteSlaveryOttomanTurksArabAndBarbaryMuslimSlaveTrade

Hanson, B. (July 14, 2020). Slavery Nearly Universal Among 'Native American' Indian Tribes Prior to White Settlement. *National Vanguard*. Retrieved from https://nationalvanguard.org/2020/07/slavery-nearly-universal-among-native-american-indian-tribes-prior-to-white-settlement/

Gilio-Whitaker, Dina. (December 15, 2020). The Untold History of Native American Enslavement. Retrieved from https://www.thoughtco.com/untold-history-of-american-indian-slavery-2477982

Gallay, Alan. (2003). Indian Slavery in the Americas. *The Gilder Lehrman Institute of American History*. Retrieved from http://ap.gilderlehrman.org/essay/indian-slavery-americas

Mintz, Steven (n.d.) Historical Context: Facts about the Slave Trade and Slavery. *The Gilder Lehrman Institute of American History*. Retrieved from https://www.gilderlehrman.org/history-resources/teaching-resource/historical-context-facts-about-slave-trade-and-slavery

Harper, Douglas (n.d.) Northern Profits from Slavery. *Colonial Slavery*. Retrieved from https://www.varsitytutors.com/earlyamerica/early-america-review/volume-8/colonial-slavery

Tree Pony (n.d.) The Slave Mentality. Retrieved from https://treepony.com/the-slave-mentality/

Jackson, Kevin (June 15, 2010) The Slave Mentality. *American Thinker*. Retrieved from https://www.americanthinker.com/articles/2010/06/the_slave_mentality.html

Johnson, Charles (n.d.) The Willie Lynch Letter and The Making of a Slave. Retrieved from https://www.saberesafricanos.net/phocadownloadpap/libros/Lets_Make_A_Slave_The_Making_Of_A_Slave.pdf

Hunter, Jenny (2009) Good Hair. HBO Films. Retrieved from https://www.youtube.com/watch?v=Qzd0Q1qfWPs

Williams, Walter E. (September 20, 2017) The Welfare State's Legacy. *Creators.com*. Retrieved from https://www.creators.com/read/walter-williams/09/17/the-welfare-states-legacy

Holland, Kimberly (November 11, 2019) What is Stockholm Syndrome and Who Does it Affect? *Healtline.com*. Retrieved from https://www.healthline.com/health/mental-health/stockholm-syndrome

Levin, M. (1997). Natural Subordination, Aristotle On. Philosophy, 72(280), 241-257. doi:10.1017/S0031819100056862

Ivy Panda. (2018, November 2). *Why Do People Tolerate Class Subordination?* Retrieved from https://ivypanda.com/essays/why-do-people-tolerate-class-subordination/

Learned Helplessness. (2015). Retrieved from http://www.britannica.com/EBchecked/topic/1380861/learned-helplessness

Theodore. (2020, June). *Victim Mentality (Definition, Examples, and Help)*. Retrieved from https://practicalpie.com/victim-mentality/

Natasha Lindstaedt. (October 20, 2023). *Authoritarianism*. Retrieved from Britannica: https://www.britannica.com/topic/neutralism

Festinger, L. (1957). *A Theory of cognitive dissonance*. Stanford, CA: Stanford University Press.

Aronson, E., & Mills, J. (1959). The effect of severity of initiation on liking for a group. *The Journal of Abnormal and Social Psychology, 59(2)*, 177.

Lacal I, Ventura R. Epigenetic Inheritance: Concepts, Mechanisms and Perspectives. Front Mol Neurosci. 2018 Sep 28;11:292. doi: 10.3389/fnmol.2018.00292. PMID: 30323739; PMCID: PMC6172332. Retrieved from: https://www.ncbi.nlm.nih.gov/pmc/articles/PMC6172332/

Utsey, Shawn, Eve P. Adams and Mark Bolden (2000) *Development and Initial Validation of the Africultural Coping Systems Inventory*. Journal of Black Psychology.

Strauss, Claudia, and Naomi Quinn (1997) *A Cognitive Theory of Cultural Meaning*. Cambridge: Cambridge University Press.

Charlotte Nickerson. (October 5, 2023) *Learned Helplessness Theory In Psychology (Seligman): Examples & Coping*. Psychology » Health Psychology retrieved from: https://www.simplypsychology.org/learned-helplessness.html

Crenshaw, Kimberlé W. (2017) "*On Intersectionality: Essential Writings*". Faculty Books. 255. https://scholarship.law.columbia.edu/books/255

Al-Faham, Hajer & Davis, Angelique & Ernst, Rose. (2019). *Intersectionality: From Theory to Practice. Annual Review of Law and Social Science*. 15. 247-265. 10.1146/annurev-lawsocsci-101518-042942.

Pema Chödrön, (September 1, 2015), *Fail, Fail Again, Fail Better: Wise Advice for Leaning into the Unknown*. Sounds True

Sherry Hamby Ph.D. (June 21, 2018) *What Is Dehumanization, Anyway?* Psychology Today. What Is Dehumanization, Anyway? | Psychology Today[1]

---

1. https://www.psychologytoday.com/us/blog/the-web-violence/201806/what-is-dehumanization-anyway

Acknowledgments

We are going to emancipate ourselves from mental slavery because whilst others might free the body, none but ourselves can free the mind. Mind is your only ruler, sovereign. The man who is not able to develop and use his mind is bound to be the slave of the other man who uses his mind.

Marcus Garvey

"I have observed this in my experience of slavery, - that whenever my condition was improved, instead of it increasing my contentment, it only increased my desire to be free, and set me to thinking of plans to gain my freedom. I have found that, to make a contented slave, it is necessary to make a thoughtless one. It is necessary to darken his moral and mental vision, and, as far as possible, to annihilate the power of reason. He must be able to detect no inconsistencies in slavery; he must be made to feel that slavery is right; and he can be brought to that only when he ceased to be a man."

Frederick Douglas

"I freed a thousand slaves. I would've freed a thousand more, if they only knew they were slaves."

Harriet Tubman

Blacks were not enslaved because they were black but because they were available. Slavery has existed in the world for thousands of years. Whites enslaved other whites in Europe for centuries before the first black was brought to the Western hemisphere. Asians enslaved Europeans. Asians enslaved other Asians. Africans enslaved other Africans, and indeed even today in North Africa, blacks continue to enslave blacks.

Thomas Sowell

There is another class of coloured people who make a business of keeping the troubles, the wrongs, and the hardships of the Negro race before the public. Having learned that they are able to make a living out of their troubles, they have grown into the settled habit of advertising their wrongs — partly because they want sympathy and partly because it pays. Some of these people do not want the Negro to lose his grievances, because they do not want to lose their jobs.

Booker T. Washington

About the Author

Ling Augustus Gramling, the author of this exploration, has a fascinating and culturally rich background that significantly shaped his early years. Born in 1969 in Saigon, Vietnam, his life began against the backdrop of a nation undergoing significant political and social upheaval. His unique heritage, with an American soldier father and a Vietnamese mother, immediately placed him at the intersection of two worlds. The historical context is crucial to understanding Ling's early life. The Vietnam conflict had profound implications for the country. Ling's father being an American soldier adds a layer of complexity to the development of his adult identity, reflecting the intricate connections between nations, communities, and families during a tumultuous period.

Ling was born into royalty which adds a dimension of his family history that contradicts sharply with the subsequent challenges they faced. The fall of Saigon, renamed Ho Chi Minh City, marked a turning point in Ling's life. The sudden and dramatic departure from Vietnam likely left an ineradicable mark on him, shaping his perspective and influencing his identity. Despite the abrupt changes and challenges, Ling's parents demonstrated resilience and determination. Growing up in a poor household, they ensured that Ling and his five siblings did not experience the harsh realities of poverty. This suggests a strong sense of familial support and unity in the face of adversity.

Ling Augustus Gramling's high school years in Germany marked a pivotal period in his life, revealing not only his academic prowess but also his latent passion for music. The relocation to Germany, where his father was stationed in 1984, added another layer to Ling's already diverse cultural background, exposing him to new experiences and opportunities.

In the academic sphere, Ling excelled, earning recognition for his achievements, including membership in the National Honor Society. His enrollment in Academically Advanced Placement classes underscored his commitment to intellectual pursuits. These accomplishments reflect not only his personal dedication to education but also the support and encouragement he likely received from his family. However, it was in the vibrant and culturally diverse environment of his high school in Germany that Ling discovered his affinity for music. Despite having participated in church and school choirs before, it wasn't until this period that he began to actively perform. This suggests a pivotal moment of self-discovery, where he realized the depth of his passion for music and its potential as a means of creative expression. He not only performed but also ventured into writing and producing music highlights the evolution of his musical journey. High school served as a fertile ground for him to hone his skills and explore the various facets of music creation. The fact that he eventually turned this passion into a profession speaks to the depth of his commitment and the talent he cultivated during these formative years.

The transition from singing in choirs to actively writing and producing music suggests a journey of self-expression and artistic exploration. Ling's high school experience not only equipped him with academic achievements but also provided him with a platform to discover and nurture his creative talents. Ling's time in high school in Germany becomes a crucial chapter in his life story, marking the intersection of his academic excellence and his burgeoning passion for music. It sets the stage for his future as a professional musician and likely played a significant role in shaping the multifaceted individual he would become.

Ling's early adult life in Germany unfolds as a period marked by personal and familial milestones. In 1992, he welcomed the birth of his daughter, a significant moment that undoubtedly brought joy and a new sense of purpose to his life. Germany is rich in its cultural tapestry and diverse environment defiantly influenced Ling's and his daughter's early experiences. One notable aspect of Ling's parenting was the commitment to raising his daughter in a bilingual environment. This was a conscious effort to instill cultural diversity and language proficiency, an endeavor that aligns with Ling's own multicultural background. The exposure to multiple languages from an early age can have lasting cognitive and linguistic benefits, shaping the way his daughter perceives and engages with the world.

Ling's daughter shared his love for math and logic adds an interesting dimension to their relationship. His value in education, intellectual pursuits, and enthusiasm for analytical thinking had passed on to his child. The daughter's early affinity for mathematical concepts, such as finding square roots and solving algebraic problems at the age of four, suggests a precocious intellect and a nurturing educational environment.

Beyond academics, Ling's pride and joy also developed a keen interest in music, mirroring her father's passion. The transmission of this artistic inclination from one generation to the next underscores the potential influence of a creative and musically enriched household. Ling's own journey in music, as previously highlighted during his high school years, likely contributed to the nurturing of this shared interest.

Ling Augustus Gramling's return to the United States in 2004 marked a significant turning point in his life, as he immersed himself in understanding the political landscape and the various agendas shaping the nation. This decision to delve into the intricacies of American politics reflects a keen awareness and a sense of responsibility to comprehend the changes that had occurred since his departure as a teenager. Believing that the country he left as a child was not the country he returned to is a profound observation and a degree of cultural and societal dissonance. Ling likely witnessed shifts in the political, social, and cultural fabric of the United States over the years. This realization may have sparked a deep introspection about the evolving nature of the nation and its implications for its citizens.

The decision to initiate a book series underscores Ling's aspiration to contribute meaningfully to public discourse and potentially catalyze societal awareness and change. Using books, as a medium, offers a platform for in-depth exploration and analysis, allowing for a nuanced discussion of complex topics that everyone seems to know but no one wants to discuss implies a willingness to confront issues that may be uncomfortable, challenging, or even taboo in public discourse.